The Voice of the Bridegroom

The Voice of the Bridegroom

THE JEWISH WEDDING
and RETURN OF CHRIST

ALASTAIR KIRK

THE VOICE OF THE BRIDEGROOM

Copyright © 2023 Alastair Kirk

Direct Scripture quotations used in this book are from the New King James Version (NKJV) of the Bible unless stated otherwise.

Cover photo: The Negev Desert, Israel
(Credit: Akhil Lincoln)

www.alastairkirk.com

ISBN: 9798853967458

Also available:

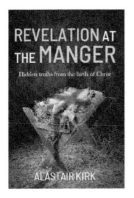

Revelation at the Manger

Revelation at the Manger uncovers the mystery of the shepherds and other hidden truths that answer who Jesus really is and why His mission and message is as relevant today as it ever has been. Alastair Kirk provides a fresh, deeper understanding of the birth of Christ, presented in a clear and concise way, challenging preconceptions and shedding new light on the miraculous account of when God sent His Son into the world.
Paperback
ISBN: 1700383051

Run the Race: Inspiration for the race of faith

Short messages from the Bible on a theme of sport and athletics encouraging us to look to Jesus who has already completed the race and wants to lead us to fulfil every potential He has for our lives.
Paperback and Kindle
ISBN: 1503378500

Dedicated to my bride, Hanna.

With special thanks to all my family for your support and to those who have invested into my life by encouraging me to seek and love the truth of the Bible.

Contents

Introduction

Thank you for choosing to read *The Voice of the Bridegroom*.

I often liken the Bible to a beautiful tapestry with layers of prophetic pictures threaded with truths to form a beautiful depiction of God's plans and purposes for mankind. There are many profound analogies to describe the relationship between God and His people. Whether it be Christ as the promised Shepherd to Israel or Him becoming a Passover Lamb for the sins of the world, there are no contradictions in the descriptions attributed to Jesus Christ, just simply a diverse portrayal of the richness of His character waiting to be explored by those wanting to get to know Him more. The same can be applied to us as His believers, referred to in roles too numerous to mention in this introduction: adopted sons, joint-heirs, servants, saints, temples of the living God, members of His Body, and the list goes on. The purpose of these spiritual metaphors has always been simple: to help us better understand the One True God and His Son, and why, when He has revealed Himself to us, His way is proven worthy of our following.

One of the most profound analogies in the Bible is the depiction of Christ being the Bridegroom and His followers, the Church, as being the Bride. It immediately suggests that there is a special relationship between Christ and the Church. It also typifies something of the love demonstrated to us by Christ. But to call it an analogy just doesn't seem to go far enough in expressing the literal way in which its concealed promises will be fulfilled.

To truly understand the meanings behind the Bride and Bridegroom picture, it is helpful to better understand aspects of the Jewish wedding, or more precisely, the Biblical marriage traditions established in ancient Israel that would be the model for Jewish weddings for generations. To this day, many of these traditions are still practiced by the Jewish people and even the contemporary Christian wedding has been influenced by these shared Biblical interpretations.

On our journey together, we will visit a Jewish wedding in the modern era, where we will recognise gems of Biblical truth. We will journey back two millennia, where we'll visit a wedding in Galilee, and we will go even further back to the Garden of Eden, where God's pattern for marriage was incepted. But we will begin our story in the arid landscape of the Negev desert, where, in answer to the prayers of Abraham's son, this beautiful picture of the Bride and Bridegroom was first painted.

It is important to go back to the foundations of Biblical marriage, because our Saviour, who was a Jew, was depicted as a bridegroom in the Jewish context. Also, our understanding of what actually defines Biblical marriage is also established in the Jewish roots of our Christian faith.

For many years I had been familiar with Jesus being described as the Bridegroom and the Church as the Bride, but when I researched this portrayal further, I realised that this analogy was just the 'tip of the ice-berg'. When I started to investigate weddings in ancient Israel from Jewish sources, I discovered so many precious Biblical truths that I became burdened to share them. Elements of the Jewish wedding that I already recognised as being fulfilled by Christ and the Church, started to fall into place piece by piece. What began as an analogy thus became a blueprint that revealed not only Christ's Covenant relationship with the Church, but also events yet to happen.

It helped me form a better understanding of the basic sequence and meaning of future prophetic events, the expectation that Christians have for Jesus's return, the destiny of Israel, and the important function that the Church has on earth today.

When I presented this message at my local church, I was asked by a visitor for my notes. The notes were adequate for my use, but my heart stirred believing that the topic warranted something more exhaustive than my basic bullet points. This was a message I wanted to share in its fullest, and so the Lord impressed upon me to write this book that I hope will be a blessing to you.

I didn't set out to write a book that was eschatologically persuasive, however the bride and bridegroom analogy is eschatological by its very nature. As we journey through this book, we will discover wonderful nuggets of truth pertaining to Christ's return and the Last Days. If you hold a theological view different to the dispensationalist view I present in this book – a view that I believe the bridegroom analogy supports – I would still urge you to read with openness and grace. The Bridegroom's promise to return for His Bride is a message too important to overlook.

But my utmost hope for this book is that you will experience a much deeper relationship with Jesus. My prayer is that you will love Him even more, lay hold onto His promises even tighter, be ready for His return with more joy, and find greater satisfaction in being part of His Bride, with a willingness to serve Him with your life.

Accompanying Study Guide

A study guide booklet to accompany *The Voice of the Bridegroom* is available for small group study or for personal notetaking. Each chapter includes points for reflection, ideas for digging deeper and group discussion starters.

Request at **www.alastairkirk.com**

"Eye has not seen, nor ear heard,
Nor have entered into the heart of man
The things which God has prepared for those
who love Him."

1 Corinthians 2:9

1

Once upon a time

*And Isaac went out to meditate in the field in the evening; and he
lifted his eyes and looked, and there, the camels were coming.
Then Rebekah lifted her eyes, and when she saw Isaac she
dismounted from her camel; for she had said to the servant, "Who
is this man walking in the field to meet us?" The servant said, "It
is my master." So she took a veil and covered herself.*
Genesis 24:63-65

It was early evening in the Negev region of the
Promised Land. In the cool of the day, as the retiring
sun transformed the arid desert landscape into a
warm glowing amber haze, Isaac made his way to a
favourite spot in one of his family's fields near *Beer
Lahai Roi.*

Just as he did at the close of every day, Isaac immersed himself in this moment of solitude to pray and contemplate. The Negev offered Isaac encompassing views from east to west and north to south, whose terrain was only broken by the scattered rusty butte or resolute desert tree. It was in this setting that Isaac removed himself from the day's demands to listen to the voice of His Creator.

Isaac was very mindful that God had spoken to his father, Abraham, many times in former days and had made special promises to him. Gazing heavenwards, the daily display of crystal lights began to slowly emerge, intensifying in brilliance and finally increasing in multitude as the indigo sky gave way to complete darkness at the full setting of the sun.

This wonder always reminded Isaac of the occasion his father fondly reminisced to Isaac when he was child. "Look upwards to the sky," God told Abraham leading him outside, "count the stars if you're able to. So shall your descendants be," (Genesis 15:5).

Growing up, Isaac had heard these words of promise retold by his father many times. His mother, Sarah, would laugh with joy at hearing her husband retell the promise at the family meal. His father's eyes would light up like the stars themselves as he recalled with excitement God's words of promise as if sharing the story for the very first time. And when journeying at night with Isaac at his side, Abraham would turn the young man's attention heavenward, pointing to the sky to remind his son of Jehovah's faithfulness.

But how could Isaac be certain that this fascinating story was different to any other his father conjured to captivate his son's imagination? As a child, Isaac often wondered curiously until an event that changed everything.

THAT day.

That heart-rendering yet glorious day on Mount Moriah, shared between Isaac and his father, that would remain etched in both their memories for the rest of their lives. It was the day that the unthinkable happened.

Obedient to His voice

After willingly accompanying his father with firewood, Isaac didn't realise that he was to be sacrificed on the altar in God's testing of Abraham. In a concoction of emotions, Abraham assured Isaac, "God himself will provide the lamb for the burnt offering."

And indeed, Jehovah provided.

Consider this unfolding picture, which is as much profound as it is familiar: The father, who loved his only son so dearly, willingly offered him as a type of atoning sacrificial lamb.

On that life-changing day, a relieved and breathless Isaac witnessed first-hand a man of great faith – his father – in much the same way that God Himself recognised in witnessing Abraham's obedience to His voice. After being spared by the angel's intervention, what happened next proved to Isaac that all his father's stories of God making promises to him were completely true. In front of the boy, an angel of the Lord spoke to his father Abraham reaffirming previous declarations that his descendants would indeed be as the stars of heaven.

"By Myself I have sworn, says the LORD, because you have done this thing, and have not withheld your son, your only son— blessing I will bless you, and multiplying I will multiply your descendants as the stars of the heaven and as the sand which is on the seashore; and your descendants shall possess the gate of their enemies. In your seed all the nations of the earth shall be blessed, because you have obeyed My voice."
Genesis 22:16-18

Descendants as the stars

As the years passed by, despite his many attempts gazing at the lights in the sky, Isaac still couldn't count the astronomical portion of God's blessing pledged to his family. Abraham's descendants, and that of Isaac's, would be multiplied to an extent unfathomable to human thinking. Today's astronomers estimate there are roughly 10,000 stars for each grain of sand on Earth. There is only One who is able to count the number of the stars and calls them all by name, as the Psalmist would one day pen (Psalm 147:4).

According to God's promise, not only would Abraham and Isaac's descendants be immeasurable, but they and their offspring would 'possess the gates' of their enemies. In other words, their descendants would be victorious against their enemies. And not only victorious, but their seed would be a blessing to all the nations of the earth, because Abraham had obeyed the voice of Almighty God.

Through the seed of Abraham and Isaac, the Jewish people would be a blessing to nations of the world both physically and spiritually. This covenant would be for all generations of their descendants and it would be everlasting (Genesis 17:7); it would be fruitful and would produce kings and nations (Genesis 17:6); it would include a Promised Land as an everlasting possession (Genesis 17:8), and He promised to be their God.

"I will make you exceedingly fruitful; and I will make nations of you, and kings shall come from you. And I will establish My covenant between Me and you and your descendants after you in their generations, for an everlasting covenant, to be God to you and your descendants after you. Also I give to you and your descendants after you the land in which you are a stranger, all the land of Canaan, as an everlasting possession; and I will be their God."
Genesis 17:6-8

And if this promise to Abraham wasn't wonderful enough in the natural, it would be through Abraham's seed that a Messiah would come to Israel, and that the blessing of Abraham would also come upon the Gentiles through faith in Him (Galatians 3:14-16). This Seed of Abraham would defeat Satan.

The first Messianic prophesy (Genesis 3:15) says that although the serpent (Satan) would bite the heel of "the woman's seed", in other words bruise and wound the Messiah, Satan would be dealt a fatal final blow and be crushed by the Seed of the woman. The Seed of Abraham, the Messiah, would be victorious.

Finding comfort

Returning to sundown in the Negev, Isaac was surrounded by land that the Lord had promised His father. The Land of Canaan was now part of Isaac's inheritance also. Everywhere Isaac looked reminded him of this covenant made between God and his father; an everlasting possession soon to be entrusted to Isaac and to generation upon generation, becoming a great nation – the nation of Israel. Isaac knew he was part of something so special.

"Remember Abraham, Isaac, and Israel, Your servants, to whom You swore by Your own self, and said to them, 'I will multiply your descendants as the stars of heaven; and all this

land that I have spoken of I give to your descendants, and they shall inherit it forever.'"
Exodus 32:13

After three years of mourning his mother's death, and with his father aging, the time had come for Isaac to find a wife by which the Bible says he would 'find comfort'. Abraham was concerned that Isaac's bride should not be from the land in which they were now strangers, but should be from his family home from which he had left.

So Abraham sent his most trusted servant to fetch a bride for his son. This servant would have been like a close aide to Abraham and even have had his own staff. His duty was to ensure that the chosen bride could easily accustom to his master's house.

"To your descendants I give this land," Abraham reminded the servant of the word that God had told him, "He will send His angel before you, and you shall take a wife for my son from there."

The servant swore an oath to Abraham, that he would indeed fetch a bride from Abraham's homeland and not from the daughter of the Canaanites. The task was so important that the servant prayed for a sign that would give him absolute clarity regarding who the right woman was to approach. With an angel going on ahead of this mission, the sign to him would be as follows: when he asks the woman for a drink of water at the well, she agrees and also offers water to his camels.

But before the servant had finished praying in his heart, a 'beautiful' young woman named Rebekah did exactly that. "Drink, my lord," Rebekah replied, followed by, "I will draw water for your camels also, until they have finished drinking."

In doing this kind act she demonstrated the admirable traits of generosity and hospitality to the servant and his camels – a sure sign of her good character. But it was also the sign that Abraham's servant had prayed for.

I will go

Abraham's servant asked if her parents might have room for him and his entourage to lodge, upon which Rebekah gladly replied that they have enough space for them to stay, plus enough straw and animal feed for the camels. In response, Abraham's servant bowed down and worshipped the Lord for answering his prayer.

When she ran home to tell her mother Bethuel, Rebekah's brother, Laban, came to meet Abraham's servant and invited him and the men who were with him into their home. There, the servant explained to Rebekah's brother and mother about Abraham, Sarah, and Isaac, and the reason for his visit to find a bride for Isaac from the land of Abraham's family. He shared how an angel had gone before him, why he had sought a sign, and how Rebekah did exactly what the Lord had prompted him to seek. Laban and Bethuel answered, "The thing comes from the Lord;

we cannot speak to you either bad or good. Here is Rebekah before you; take her and go, and let her be your master's son's wife, as the Lord has spoken."

And again Abraham's servant fell to the ground and worshipped Jehovah for His provision.

You can read this account in full in Genesis 24, but two very significant things took place following the agreement by Rebekah's family. They are significant, because their meaning and purpose will be revealed later in this book.

Firstly, Abraham's servant brought out silver and gold jewellery and clothing as gifts to Rebekah and also to her bother and mother. Then a very crucial component of the process took place. We read that Rebekah wasn't forced, but rather gave her personal agreement to the proposal. The family wanted to delay Rebekah's departure for 10 days, but Abraham's servant insisted that now was the time. Genesis 24:57 tells us the family's response: "'We will call the young woman and ask her personally,' then they called Rebekah and said to her, 'Will you go with this man?' And she said, 'I will go.'"

After Rebekah's consent was given, her sisters blessed her saying,

> *"Our sister, may you become*
> *The mother of thousands of ten thousands;*
> *And may **your descendants possess**
> **The gates** of those who hate them."*
> Genesis 24:60

25

Possessing the gates

These precious words uttered by Rebekah's sisters make a remarkable connection with the promise of blessing that God gave Abraham in Genesis 22 after his act of faith on Mount Moriah. For in both the covenant to Abraham and blessing upon Rebekah, we read the phrase about possessing the gate of the enemy.

In the most incredible way, the blessing poured upon Rebekah prophetically points to her destined role in the Abrahamic covenant, when it states, "may your descendants possess the gates of those who hate them."

Not only is this phrase stated in the promise to Abraham (Genesis 22), but it is even more profound when we consider it was given by God in direct response to Abraham's obedience and willingness to sacrifice his only son, Isaac. Now, years later, God's promise to multiply his descendants "as the stars of the heaven and the sand on the seashore" was about to fall into place through the union of Rebekah and his spared son, Isaac.

The 'gates of the enemy', shared in both Rebekah's and Abraham's blessings, was an expression used in ancient times that meant to have control over your enemy. The gates were a strategic target for breaching the enemy's stronghold.

By the fulfilment of God's promise to Abraham and his descendants, God's chosen people would overcome their enemies. Not even Israel's enemies could derail God's covenant from being fulfilled. What a comforting reminder that those who 'hate the descendants' of Isaac and Rebekah – those throughout history and those in the present and future – will be humbled when Israel has final victory over its enemies.

The enemy's defeat

And in a spiritual sense, the seed of Abraham would lead to the greatest defeat of the enemy of God – Jesus Christ's victory over Satan.

In fulfilment of the everlasting promises of God's Word, the promised Messiah, Jesus Christ, descendant of Isaac and Rebekah, would bring triumph over death and power over sin through His death on the Cross and victory over the grave.

Every person who puts their trust in the God of Israel will also 'possess the gate of the enemy'. In other words, the schemes of Satan will not succeed. The gates have been breached. God has equipped us with the strategic means by which to overcome the enemy. Strongholds have been torn down. The 'gates of hell' shall not prevail.

God's purpose through the union of Isaac and Rebekah was set to change history.

I bow down and worship, like Abraham's servant, in thanksgiving that God has fulfilled His Word. God is faithful to keep His promises to me, just as He keeps His everlasting promises to Israel. I am a partaker in the promise that Christ has triumphed over Satan. I confess that I will 'possess the gates' of those who are against me and that the enemies of Jehovah will not succeed. I trust in the God of Abraham, Isaac and Jacob and receive His blessings in my life, for my family, and for generations to come.

2

The Covenant

The real love story of the Bible is revealed to us when we have revelation of God's love for His people. We see this in the form of His love for Israel, His love for the world (John 3:16) and His love for the Church. Follow the traces of this great love story and you will discover God's great love for *you*.

At the basis of God's love is His faithfulness to keep *all* His promises. The covenant Jehovah made with Abraham, Isaac, Jacob, and their descendants is an everlasting one. God has not forsaken His promise to the Jewish people – His promise for them to become a great nation – neither has He withdrawn their everlasting inheritance or blessings.

So many times we read in the Scriptures how 'God remembered His covenant with Abraham' because the Lord is faithful to keep His Word. It was and still is God's will for His people to remain in relationship with Him.

Another covenant God made with His people is sometimes called the Covenant of the Law, or Mosaic Covenant, because it was given to Moses. This didn't supersede the covenant God made with Abraham, but provided a way for Israel to enjoy the full extent of blessings that God has for His chosen people.

The problem Israel had was that in practice their unholiness was incompatible with a Holy God. Their unfaithfulness was an offense to a faithful God. Their rebelliousness challenged the integrity of His promised blessings. Therefore, the Law that God gave to Moses was the basis upon which God dealt with His people in the Land He promised them. Notably, it provided a method for sinful people to remain in communion with a righteous God, but only temporarily.

It was by the specific animal sacrifices described in the Torah that the covenant of the Law remained intact between God and His people. The nation's sin could only be temporarily covered by the shedding of blood at the altar, hence why it had to be continually repeated.

Not only was the Law a reflection of God's holiness by which those who fear Him were called to live by, but Israel's continual breaking of the law exposed every human-being's inability to keep it.

Only One person has ever lived that could keep the Law perfectly because He was sinless. This person is Jesus Christ. Despite being without sin, the

Bible says that He *became* sin for us, giving His life as a living sacrifice on the Cross, so that those who have broken God's Law (sinners) can find His forgiveness once and for all!

"For He made Him who knew no sin to be sin for us, that we might become the righteousness of God in Him."
2 Corinthians 5:21

Not with the blood of goats and calves, but with His own blood He entered the Most Holy Place once for all, having obtained eternal redemption.
Hebrews 9:12

Prophesied by Jeremiah as a 'new covenant' (Jeremiah 31:31-33), we see it unfold before our eyes when we read the account in the New Testament of God sending His Son to save sinners. The prophecy of Jeremiah 31 is cited in the New Testament book of Hebrews:

For if that first covenant had been faultless, then no place would have been sought for a second. Because finding fault with them, He says: "Behold, the days are coming, says the Lord, when I will make a new covenant with the house of Israel and with the house of Judah—not according to the covenant that I made with their fathers in the day when I took them by the hand to lead them out of the land of Egypt; because they did not continue in

My covenant, and I disregarded them, says the Lord. For this is the covenant that I will make with the house of Israel after those days, says the Lord: I will put My laws in their mind and write them on their hearts; and I will be their God, and they shall be My people.
Hebrews 8:7-10

The 'law of God', which we can describe as God's righteousness, was now 'written' on the heart of the believer in Jesus Christ. God's righteousness was no longer achieved outwardly and temporarily, but was fulfilled inwardly and permanently by the saving blood of Jesus Christ.

For sin shall not have dominion over you, for you are not under law but under grace.
Romans 6:14

The powerful imagery of Jesus taking the 'cup of the new covenant' on the night before He died is a reminder of the new relationship that is enjoyed by those that accept this gift of saving grace.

For by grace you have been saved through faith, and that not of yourselves; it is the gift of God.
Ephesians 2:8

New relationship

From the cup flows new life in Jesus, the washing away of sin, the cleansing power of His forgiveness, the promise of an eternal inheritance, and the entering into a personal relationship with a Holy God. By this 'new covenant', Jesus becomes our 'mediator'. This means it is possible for you and me to remain *in covenant* with God continually through His death and resurrection. Furthermore, we can call upon Him directly and at any time.

God wants to be *in relationship* with you because He is a covenant-making God. He has special blessings for you. And importantly, He wants you to experience the full extent of His blessings in your life.

His love is immeasurable. His mercy is enduring. His grace is sufficient. His favour is unmerited. His forgiveness heals our brokenness. His compassion never fails.

And for this reason He is the Mediator of the new covenant, by means of death, for the redemption of the transgressions under the first covenant, that those who are called may receive the promise of the eternal inheritance.
Hebrews 9:15

Your people shall be my people

As already highlighted, when considering God's covenants, we must begin by acknowledging that the

God of Israel chose the physical seed of Abraham, Isaac and Jacob (the Jewish people) as the custodians of His law and the recipients of His covenants and their associated blessings. Meanwhile, Gentiles (non-Jews) have been granted the opportunity to become partakers of these blessings through the New Covenant we have just described.

Before we discover truths from the ancient Jewish wedding, let us visit another love story in the Scriptures.

A young Moabite woman named Ruth suddenly found herself widowed along with her mother-in-law Naomi, a Jew, after their respective husbands died. Ruth's marriage had been an unholy alliance because the Moabites had tried to curse the Israelites as they journeyed to enter the Promised Land. Therefore, the Law prohibited Jews from marrying Moabites.

Naomi tried to persuade her daughter-in-law Ruth to remain in her native Moab just as her other daughter-in-law, Orpah, had decided to do, and Naomi would return to Judah. But the Bible says Ruth 'clung' to Naomi, in contrast to Oprah. The word 'clung' in Hebrew is the same word used for marriage.

Ruth was not only a woman of faith and grace, but her promise before God bound her to willingly remain with her mother-in-law, who was now alone.

In fact Ruth's commitment to Naomi is expressed in her own words in this memorable passage:

But Ruth said:
> *"Entreat me not to leave you,*
> *Or to turn back from following after you;*
> *For wherever you go, I will go;*
> *And wherever you lodge, I will lodge;*
> *Your people shall be my people,*
> *And your God, my God.*
> *Where you die, I will die,*
> *And there will I be buried.*
> *The LORD do so to me, and more also,*
> *If anything but death parts you and me."*
> Ruth 2:16-20

Here was a young Gentile woman, deciding to make the God of Israel her God and the people of Israel her people. It is illustrative of God's special plan in providing Gentiles with the open invitation to worship the God of Abraham, Isaac and Jacob and provide a means to enter into covenant with Him through faith in Jesus Christ. To lay aside the gods made on our own accord. To reject the gods created out of our ignorance, pride and rebellion, and choosing instead to follow the God of Israel unreservedly. Recognising with gratitude the special connection Christians have with the Jewish people, it is as if to say, "your God shall be my God."

Fast forward to her arrival in Naomi's home-town, it was in the grain fields of *Bet Lehem* (Bethlehem), meaning 'House of Bread', that one of the Bible's fondest love stories occurred. Gathering grain for harvest, it was here that Ruth met her future bridegroom, Boaz. Ruth's love-match with Boaz is a story you can read in the book of Ruth.

Her decision to listen to God's voice in her life led to her becoming the great-grandmother of King David. After they were married, Ruth became pregnant and gave birth to a son named Obed, and then became grandmother to Obed's son, Jesse. It was among these same fields of *Bet Lehem* that Samuel was led by the Lord to choose Jesse's son, David, to anoint him King of Israel. This 'house of bread' was also the setting of God's provision to the world, culminating in the 'Son of David', the 'bread of life', Jesus Christ being born.

This Gentile woman, who feared the Lord and made Jehovah her God, is honoured in the genealogy of Jesus at the beginning of the book of Matthew.

I invite you now to join me as we continue to look at elements of the traditional Jewish wedding. If, like Ruth, you have decided to follow the One True God, the precious truths we will uncover are for YOU!

Thank you, Lord, for your abundant grace and the gift of righteousness. You have written your law in my heart and I am being changed into the person that You have created me to be. Like Ruth, I will not be defined by the person I once was, or the person the enemy might want me to say I am. I have chosen to follow the One True God, and have received new life through His Son, the Bread of Life. I am not the sinner I once was. I am forgiven. I have been set free. I am a participant in the New Covenant and have relationship with the Father through the power of the blood of Jesus Christ.

Waterpot in Cana, Israel

3

The best is yet to come

Let us return to the land of Canaan, where Isaac is praying in the field near *Beer Lahai Roi*, which means, 'the well of him that lives and sees me', or 'the well of the vision of life'.

This special place in the Negev was the location that God had first told Abraham that he would have children.

Isaac had made it his daily practice to pray in the same spot near *Beer Lahai Roi* each evening just before sunset. Isaac's routine has since inspired what is known as the *Mincha* afternoon prayer service, one of the five Jewish daily prayers.

On this particular occasion, Isaac's life and the course of history was about to change. As Isaac was dedicating time to praying and introspection, the Bible says that he looked up and saw camels on the horizon – his father's camels. This convoy of camels included Abraham's servant and his men, and Rebekah and her maids. As they approached, Rebekah noticed a lonely figure rise to his feet and walk towards them. The Bible says she 'lifted her eyes'. The phrase suggests something remarkable happened deep within her emotions, compelling her to dismount from her camel – in fact the word in Hebrew suggests almost throwing herself off the camel.

As Isaac started walking towards them, she inquired of the servant about who this approaching man was. Being told it was her bridegroom, she immediately veiled her face as was the custom.

The Negev Desert, Israel

The blueprint begins

The union between Isaac and Rebekah not only provided the continuation of God's covenant with His chosen people, but also became the blueprint for the traditional Jewish wedding ceremony. These ancient traditions were passed from generation to generation, and whilst new traditions were added to Jewish weddings over time, the model laid out in Genesis 24 remains foundational to this day. In fact, traditions associated with Christian weddings in some cultures are also traceable to these same customs.

In the traditional Jewish wedding ceremony, still widely practiced today, before the bride and bridegroom stand under the chuppah (a cloth canopy under which the couple stand for the ceremony), the bridegroom is led *to* the bride, as opposed to the bride being taken to the bridegroom. When he sees her, he covers her face with a veil just like Rebekah covered her face. Significantly, it is usually *only* in the presence of the bridegroom that the veiling takes place, just as Rebekah had waited until being in the presence of Isaac before putting on her veil. Some say that the bridegroom places the veil himself to avoid a repeat of the deception and confusion that Laban caused Jacob in tricking him to marry Leah instead of Rachel.

As the bridegroom places the veil onto his bride, he recites the same blessing over the bride that Rebekah's family recited over her before she departed.

"*Achotenu: at hayi le alfei revavah* — Our sister, be thou the mother of thousands of ten thousands."

These are just a few examples of how Genesis 24 forms the basis of the ancient Jewish wedding traditions. But there is still much more that we will discover.

Cana, Galilee

Let us fast forward to First-Century A.D.

Taking place at a home among the green rolling hills of the lower Galilee, celebrations are in full flow at a Jewish wedding banquet. There is great rejoicing, plentiful feasting and jubilant dancing – lots of dancing! But there is a problem. All seems to be going smoothly until word spread that the wine had run dry. The celebrations were drawing to a close after several days, but the honour of the family was now on the line unless something was done to replenish the empty wine vessels.

I'm referring, of course, to the wedding attended by Jesus in Cana, recorded in John chapter 2. The wedding was either that of a family member, relative, or close family friend of Jesus. Jesus's disciples were in attendance, his mother Mary, and even Jesus's brothers, as inferred by verse 12.

It was Mary who alerted Jesus to the crisis. John 2:3-4 states:

And when they ran out of wine, the mother of Jesus said to Him, "They have no wine."

Jesus said to her, "Woman, what does your concern have to do with Me? My hour has not yet come."

It wasn't the first occasion that Jesus had reminded His mother of His Kingdom calling. He was only a child when he was found sitting among the teachers in the Temple, where He told His anxious mother and father, "Why did you seek Me? Did you not know that I must be about My Father's business?"

Now, almost two decades later, Jesus was reminding his mother that "His hour has not yet come."

What 'hour' was this referring to? Jesus was referring to the 'hour' – the occasion – for which He would die and rise again. We know from Mary's interaction with the Bethlehem shepherds, and 40 days later in her encounter with Simeon and Anna at the Temple, that Mary knew something of her son's destiny. But Jesus's answer, referring to His death and resurrection, in response to what seemed like a trivial crisis over drinks supply, suggests that this request by Mary carried a deeper significance.

Jesus performed many miracles that were movements of compassion, but Jesus's initial reaction to the wine crisis doesn't immediately convey this feeling. I don't believe He was simply responding with sympathy to spare the host's embarrassment. Rather, something took place at this feast that Jesus used as a profound moment to launch His powerful ministry.

Jesus's ministry had only just begun. Until now the Bible doesn't record any previous miracles by Jesus, suggesting that this was His first. Jesus had just been baptised by John the Baptist, at which the Spirit of God had come upon Him like a dove and the voice of the Father had proclaimed, "This is My beloved Son, in whom I am well pleased."

This was the beginning of Jesus's ministry that would lead to 'His hour' being fulfilled – an event that would be world-changing. Was Mary aware of the significance of Jesus's encounter with God the Father that had recently taken place in the River Jordan? And was this why she now approached her son with such strong faith, believing that He was able to work a miracle? It may have been a simple mother's confidence in her son's ability and willingness, but the timing seems to suggest that Mary was prompting Jesus to initiate what would be the first of many miracles.

It is also fitting that Jesus's first miracle should take place at a wedding feast, as Biblically weddings symbolise the beginning of a new period. In this case, it was the beginning of Jesus's ministry that would culminate at the Cross.

The Bible says that what Jesus did next was a 'sign'. The word for 'sign' in John 2:11 is *semeion*, which is translated 'miracle' in some English translations, but it literally means 'a sign, mark, or signal'. John uses this word seven times in relation to what we might more commonly refer to as miracles. It was as if these miracles were deliberate 'markers' or 'signals' that pointed to, or confirmed, very important events fulfilled through the work of Christ in the Gospels. When considering Jesus's miracles, we should take special note of those that are described as a 'sign'. In this case, John 2:11 says that it was the "beginning of signs that Jesus did in Cana of Galilee" to "manifest His glory" and cause His disciples to believe in Him.

So, this miracle was the first of 'signs'; it was at a wedding, symbolic of new beginnings; it was very soon after Jesus's baptism; His mother Mary's approach caused Jesus to refer to something that seemed much more serious than what otherwise seemed like a trivial matter. Bearing all of these things in mind, let us continue with what Jesus did next.

Mary told the servants to do whatever Jesus asked them to do (John 2:5). The Bible tells us that there were six stone waterpots that were used for 'purification of the Jews'. These were often set in their special place, front and centre at a Jewish feast so that guests could cleanse themselves.

There were also waterpots set aside privately for the bride and her family to use separately from the guests. We don't know which waterpots were used specifically, but Jesus told the servants to "fill the waterpots with water." The Bible actually says that they filled them to the brim. This was to prevent any possibility of them being diluted, thus avoiding any suspicion of trickery or the deception of watered-down wine. With the water having miraculously turned into wine, the servants themselves presented some to the master of ceremonies and he was astounded:

> *"When the master of the feast had tasted the water that was made wine, and did not know where it came from (but the servants who had drawn the water knew), the master of the feast called the bridegroom."*
> John 2:9

Why did the master of ceremonies call the bridegroom? The reason is because the one person who was ultimately responsible for the provision of wine at the wedding was the bridegroom! In fact, it was considered honourable for the bridegroom to plentifully sustain his guests with the adequate provision of the wine. In other words, it was the bridegroom's role and *only* his. Therefore, the bridegroom was to be blamed for not adequately ensuring that there was enough wine.

It is possible to read the miracle at the wedding in Cana and miss the following important truth. When Jesus turned the water into wine – something that we have already established was the 'first of signs' – it is important to realise that Jesus momentarily stepped into the role of bridegroom to deliver what the actual bridegroom was expected to provide for the wedding guests.

This special occasion that marked Jesus's first miracle saw Him deliver a sign that symbolically placed Him in the function of bridegroom at the feast.

The best is yet to come

But what Jesus provided wasn't a direct substitute for the wine that had previously run dry. Many people over time have speculated about the type of wine that Jesus provided, or even whether it was wine at all, as if we are connoisseurs of what the world considers important. We are not. We are only enthusiasts of God's truth. And the truth is that the water that was filled to the brim was supernaturally touched by the Lord of hosts.

The Bridegroom (uppercase B) had supplied 'the best'.

> *And he said to him, "Every man at the beginning sets out the good wine, and when the guests have well drunk, then the inferior. You have kept the good wine until now!"*
> John 2:10

Traditionally, the best wine was always set out first to give the best impression to the guests. As the feast progressed, satisfied guests became less fussy about what filled their cups, hence why the least impressive and often even diluted wine was distributed last.

With Jesus in attendance, the best wine was yet to come. The Bridegroom intervened at a crucial moment and provided something that the guests had not experienced until right at the very end. And so it will be when Christ returns. The best is yet to come.

Jesus's provision is above and beyond anything the world can offer. Any worry today about what we lack, physically or spiritually, can be resolved by inviting Jesus to intervene. Our spiritual emptiness or any other need can be met by the supernatural provision of the Lord Jesus, who we can call upon and who can be depended.

What should our first step be to see the Lord's hand move? As Mary told the servants, "Whatever He says to you, do it."

Whatever he says, do it

Such simple words, spoken so softly yet assuredly. Not embroiled in religious conditions. Not loaded with questions such as are you ready, how strong is your faith, or have you ever seen water turned into wine? Just a command directed with confidence, "Do anything he tells you."

This is the simplicity of following Christ's instructions. Do as He says. This doesn't mean what is being asked is easy. It inevitability requires choosing the narrow way through obedience to Him. But those who *do* accept His invitation can testify that His way is best.

Listen to the voice of the Bridegroom. Let us come to Him with our empty waterpots, with simple obedience and draw upon what the Bridegroom has in store for us.

Our search in satisfying our desires in this world pale in comparison with what Christ has in store for those who trust in Him. This is the 'sign' to us as His disciples today – that His glory is manifested and that we might 'believe in Him'.

> *I invite the Bridegroom to intervene in my life today. I bring my needs before Jesus as ask Him to undertake. Help me, Lord, to listen to the voice of the Bridegroom. Place within my heart a desire to do what He says. I come before Him with an empty waterpot. Fill me, Lord, as I draw upon your provision in my life. Thank You, Lord, that the best is yet to come.*

4

The cup

It is no coincidence that Jesus chose a wedding to perform His first miracle. In fact, the Bible begins and ends with marriage. After all, the first marriage union didn't originate in the dusty, arid plains of the Negev, but rather among the verdant fauna of the Garden of Eden.

In the perfect realm of God's Creation, before the Fall, God saw that everything was good, except one thing: He observed that it wasn't good for man to be alone. So He created a woman using one of his ribs (Genesis 2:21). It says in Genesis 2:23:

And Adam said,
'This is now bone of my bones
And flesh of my flesh;

She shall be called Woman,
Because she was taken out of Man."

The Biblical concept of marriage was founded at this point. It was a concept ordained by God Himself, not only to establish the personal relationship between Adam and Eve, but to set God's blueprint for humanity for generations to come. This is evident in the next verse (Genesis 2:24), where we read:

Therefore a man shall leave his father and mother and be joined to his wife, and they shall become one flesh.

The word 'therefore' introduces the idea of a man leaving his father and mother to be joined to his wife, based upon God's Creation of woman out of man in the preceding verse. The order of marriage was curated at this moment, despite Adam and Eve not having a father and mother of their own to leave, and before they were a father and mother themselves. Importantly, this means God's pattern for marriage was original Creation design, originating from before the Fall, not an institution established after to accommodate man's fallen state.

The solemnity of marriage was also presented to us with the revelation that man and woman, related in part by the mystery of the rib, would become united and complete as 'one flesh'.

The institution of marriage was divinely created by the Creator and reaffirmed by Jesus Christ

Himself. Jesus replied to the Pharisees in Matthew 19:4-5:

Have you not read that He who made them at the beginning 'made them male and female,' and said, 'For this reason a man shall leave his father and mother and be joined to his wife, and the two shall become one flesh'?

The final marriage mentioned in the Bible is described in Revelation 19:

"Let us be glad and rejoice and give Him glory, for the marriage of the Lamb has come, and His wife has made herself ready."
Revelation 19:7

We will return later to the marriage described in the book of Revelation. It will be the biggest and most important wedding feast in the history of the universe. No one should want to miss it.

If God institutes something, we need to give it our full attention. No wonder Jesus chose a wedding to launch His life-changing ministry.

I now invite you to come with me to a First-Century Jewish wedding ceremony typical of the time during Jesus's earthly life. When we understand that the Bible describes Jesus Christ as the Bridegroom and those that believe in Him as 'His Bride', references to the Jewish wedding in the Bible take on powerful new meaning.

We have only just begun our discovery of the greatest love story ever. A love story that includes you and me. A discovery that will deepen your understanding of God's unfolding plans and strengthen your faith. Just as Jehovah counts the number of the stars, He is mindful of His Covenant towards His people and a keeper of His everlasting promises.

The marriage structure, based on the Biblical pattern for Jewish weddings in ancient Israel, can be divided into seven parts.

The covenant

The betrothal

The Preparation of the Bride

The Preparation of the Bridegroom

The Bridegroom fetches the Bride

The consummation of the marriage

The wedding feast

The covenant

In Bible times, when a young man wanted to marry a young woman, he had to prepare a special contract, or covenant, known as a ***ketubah*** in Jewish law. The man would take it in person to the woman's family home to meet with her and her father. So, the soon-to-be bridegroom leaves his father's house and travels to the bride's home. The groom presents the terms under which he would propose marriage and express his willingness to provide.

Included in these terms is a central component of the proposal – the *bride purchase price*, which was in exchange for permission to marry. This practice may seem somewhat alien to those of us in a Western culture. Over time, the tradition became more symbolic, almost as a customary role-play in the ceremony, but it is a very important part of the contract.

Until now, the woman had been under the covering of her father and therefore it wasn't simply a matter of her breaking that tie to be joined with her husband. The woman's father needed to see evidence that she was worth something very valuable to the young man. And equally the man would have wanted to demonstrate how valuable she was to him. This bride-price was called a **mohar** and was traditionally given by the man's father to the father of the woman. It was also tradition in Bible times for the woman's father to in turn pass on a portion of the bride-price to his daughter.

The reality is that a daughter is invaluable to a loving father. And a father hopes to see that his daughter is regarded as precious to her suiter. That is why the *mohar* was more about the sacrificial heart of the bridegroom than the price itself.

A *mohar* wasn't always paid in money. Sometimes it was paid in kind or in service. In the account of Isaac and Rebekah, it says the servant of Abraham "brought out silver and gold jewellery and clothing as a gift to Rebekah and also to her brother and mother."

These gifts to Rebekah's brother and mother were part of the *mohar*. Meanwhile, the gifts given to Rebekah are known in Hebrew as **mattan**. The *mattan* is different to the *mohar*, because it was a personal gift from the young man to his bride as opposed to the gifts to her family. Historically, the *mattan* was anything from a prayer book to a piece of fruit, a property deed, or a special wedding coin.

Whilst the tradition of giving a ring to the bride was introduced in Judaism much later (dates vary between 8th and 10th Century in Judaism and much earlier in other cultures), the ring very much embraces this custom of giving a precious gift to the bride.

The betrothal

You may be asking, "What if the woman didn't want to marry the man?" In real life it would have been common for families to make arrangements prior to the customary *ketubah*. One can easily imagine a scenario of fathers of young women being approached by eligible bachelors, and at the same time fathers would be looking to marry off their daughters. But no marriage could happen without the consent of the woman. Therefore, this intention was far from being a 'forced-marriage', which is certainly not based on the Biblical blueprint. In fact, the woman's consent to agreeing to the marriage is one of the most powerful images involved in the marriage covenant. This traces back to the story in Genesis 24 where Rebekah had to agree to leaving her family to marry Isaac.

The passage says that Rebekah's family, specifically her "mother and brothers", asked Rebekah whether she consented to leave and marry Isaac.

"'We will call the young woman and ask her personally,' then they called Rebekah and said to her, 'Will you go with this man?' And she said, 'I will go.'"

This provides an interesting insight into the family's role in this situation. Whilst a caring father would check and approve the *bridegroom's* suitability, it took a caring mother's love to reach out and probe the heart of the *bride* herself. Equally, it took the role of protective brothers to inquire of the bride's contentment at leaving and entering marriage.

There was one further act that was needed to seal the covenant – the most important and profound step at this initial stage of the marriage. This ratifying of the covenant between a young man and woman is called the **erusin** in Hebrew, translated 'betrothal'. Today, it translates as 'engagement', but this isn't a completely accurate definition of what *erusin* represents Biblically and traditionally. It is also referred to as **kiddushin,** meaning 'sanctification or dedication'.

After the bride-price had been agreed by the father, the bridegroom would pour a glass of wine for her. He would then take the cup and place it on a table between them. This cup is the new covenant that would be established between them.

The woman now has a decision to make. She can either take the cup that is being offered her or reject it. The choice was hers. If she declined the cup, she would be effectively rejecting the bridegroom and no covenant would be made. There would be no relationship. The price would be null and void.

But to accept the young man as her bridegroom, she would need to take the cup and drink it. At the very moment she drank the wine in the cup a benediction blessing was proclaimed and they became betrothed.

Fulfilment

"Then He took the cup, and gave thanks, and gave it to them, saying, "Drink from it, all of you. For this is My blood of the new covenant, which is shed for many for the remission of sins."
Matthew 26:27-28

Friend, a cup of covenant has been provided by Jesus, the Bridegroom. This cup has been placed 'for many' for the forgiveness of sin. It is on the table for us to receive. And this is an offer every person is invited to accept.

Like an artist painting layers of colour onto canvas, a picture begins to emerge of the Biblical wedding and its link with the mission of the Lord Jesus Christ.

Jesus left the home of His Father in Heaven to come to the home of His prospective Bride on earth to purchase her for a price. As Bridegroom, the price was something that demonstrated His deep compassion for the Bride. When you understand this cost, you will understand the affection and commitment that the Son has for you. And the extent to which you are chosen to be grafted into His family.

And yet you may wonder why a price was even needed at all. The Bible says in 1 Corinthians 7:23 that you have been bought at a price. Acts 20:28 says that the "church of God" has been "purchased with His own blood."

This aligns the Church with the picture of the Bride, purchased with the precious blood of Jesus. It is through the shedding of Christ's blood at Calvary that believers in Him, that is the Bride of Christ, can enter into covenant with God. It is through His blood that the price for our sins has been paid. Jesus paid the bride-price by laying down His life.

There is no greater means by which the Bride of Christ could be purchased. There is no greater value to express His love for the Church.

When Jesus came to earth, the world was presented with a type of 'marriage contract'. The marriage contract provided by Jesus is the New Covenant, which is presented in the Gospels as the means by which it has been made possible for us to receive the forgiveness of sins.

On the night before He died, Jesus shared the Passover meal with His disciples. Passover is the Biblical feast to remember God sparing the Israelites in Egypt after they obeyed Him by placing the blood of a lamb on the doorposts of their homes. After supper, the Bible says in 1 Corinthians 11 that Jesus broke bread to remind His followers of His body broken for them, instructing them and all followers of Him to continue to do likewise in remembrance of Him. Next, a cup of red wine was placed before the disciples with the following words from Jesus:

"This cup is the new covenant in My blood. This do, as often as you drink it, in remembrance of Me."

Just as the young woman had the choice to accept the cup poured out for her, the disciples had a choice to accept the cup being offered by Jesus. Today when followers of Jesus take the cup in the Lord's Supper, sometimes called 'communion', they do so to remember the sacrifice by Jesus shedding His blood on the Cross. The participant also takes the cup as a reflection of Christ's saving work that has already taken place inside the heart of the believer upon their decision to accept Christ into their lives.

As you are reading this, you have this same choice to receive the cup placed on the table – the cup offered by Jesus's sacrifice on the Cross. If you accept this cup, you are acknowledging the great price that has been paid for the forgiveness of your sin.

If we look more closely at the Passover supper, we understand that there was in fact more than one cup in accordance with Exodus 6:6-7. The cup taken after supper was traditionally the third cup, known as the 'Cup of Deliverance'. When Jesus announced this cup as the 'New Covenant of His blood', He effectively made reference to the promise of Jeremiah 31 in which God declared that He would make a new covenant with His people.

If you have taken this cup, metaphorically speaking, then you have entered into this New Covenant with Jesus Christ. Devastatingly, there are many people that have rejected the cup that has been willingly offered, but it's there for you to take and receive as a free gift that brings you into a life-changing personal relationship with Jesus Christ.

The Bride of Christ is not an individual, but every believer purchased by the blood of Jesus Christ. The reason we share the bread and the cup when we participate in the Lord's Supper is to acknowledge that we are part of the Body of Christ, which the Bible also describes as the Church.

Remember, it wasn't only the bride that receives the cup of wine. The bridegroom also drinks of the cup. It is really important to understand this point. There would be no Covenant if the Bridegroom, Jesus, hadn't drunk the cup Himself. This reminds me of Luke chapter 22, moments before Jesus's arrest, where our Lord was in the Garden of

Gethsemane, toiling with the immense magnitude of what He was about to face. Kneeling in prayer and 'in agony', Jesus said, "Father, if it is Your will, take this cup away from Me; nevertheless not My will, but Yours, be done."

Then it says an angel appeared and "strengthened Him".

The cup on offer to you today is possible because Jesus was willing to take the cup in obedience to the Father.

The outcome of betrothal

Returning to the Jewish wedding, at the point of betrothal the marriage contract was formalised. But this was only the first part of the wedding ceremony.

From this point forward, the bride and bridegroom would be separated. The bride was sanctified, or set apart, exclusively for her bridegroom. And the bridegroom would depart to his father's house to prepare a place for his bride.

Lord, I thank You for your body that was broken for me. I thank you for the Cup of the New Covenant, shed for the forgiveness of my sin. In remembrance of Your sacrifice, I receive the cup presented to me with appreciation in my heart for laying down Your life for me. Because Jesus drank from the cup, the price has been paid. I am a redeemed child of God. I am saved and sanctified by the cleansing power of the blood of Jesus.

5

Preparation of the Bridegroom

"Let not your heart be troubled; you believe in God, believe also in Me. In My Father's house are many mansions; if it were not so, I would have told you. I go to prepare a place for you. And if I go and prepare a place for you, I will come again and receive you to Myself; that where I am, there you may be also. And where I go you know, and the way you know."
John 14:1-4

The cup of betrothal was a symbol of the covenant between the bride and the bridegroom that would last until the bridegroom's return. Until then, the cup represented the precious promise that her bridegroom would in due time come back to take her for himself.

When Jesus instituted the partaking of the Lord's Supper, He gave clear instruction that His followers were to repeat the ordinance in remembrance of Him *until* He returns.

It states in 1 Corinthians 11:25-26:

"In the same manner He also took the cup after supper, saying, 'This cup is the new covenant in My blood. This do, as often as you drink it, in remembrance of Me. For as often as you eat this bread and drink this cup, you proclaim the Lord's death till He comes.'"

The communion cup is not only a symbolic depiction of the power of Jesus's sacrifice and the blessing of His precious new covenant, it is also a reminder that Jesus, who defeated sin and death by rising again, will in fact return. Jesus tells us to not stop remembering. For similar reasons to why God commanded the Jewish people to observe the Passover from one generation to the next, the Lord's Supper – which Jesus actually shared with His disciples at the Passover meal on the night before He died – was to serve as a permanent reminder to His followers that God has provided a perfect Lamb to take away the sins of the world.

When believers in Jesus Christ take the cup, we "proclaim the Lord's death" until He returns. We proclaim His sacrifice for each of us; we declare His forgiveness and grace poured out at Calvary, and we pronounce His power over sin and death accomplished on that miracle day. His resurrection on the third day gives us complete confidence that the power of the Cross is proven. And His ascension to Heaven and His promise to return in the same manner as He departed is a comfort that He *will* return.

Separation

At the point of the Jewish couple's betrothal, the bridegroom and the bride are separated from one another. A commitment has been formalised, a relationship has been created, and a promise has been proclaimed. But to the couple's sadness, they now have to come to terms with a difficult period of lengthy separation. The bride remains at her family home and the bridegroom returns to his father's house. The two will then begin to separately prepare for their marriage. Their respective preparations are quite different.

We will begin by looking at the preparation by the bridegroom.

It might come as a surprise to some that as His Bride, believers in Christ are to prepare for Jesus's return. We will look at this in the next chapter. But some may be even more surprised that Jesus is also making preparation for *His* return. But how is Jesus preparing?

Amazingly, Jesus Himself told us exactly what He is doing between departing this earth and before His return. In fact, what He described to His disciples prior to his death fits perfectly into the pattern of the betrothal.

In ancient Jewish tradition, the bridegroom created special quarters inside his father's house in preparation for taking his bride to commence their marriage. Amazingly, it is this custom that provides a shadow of what will happen when Christ returns for His Bride.

Reserved for you!

The Bible says that the Son is right now preparing many rooms in His Father's house for the saints who are part of the Bride of Christ. Jesus referred to this as an analogy when speaking to His disciples, when He said,

> *"In My Father's house are many mansions; if it were not so, I would have told you. I go to prepare a place for you. And if I go and prepare a place for you, I will come again and receive you to Myself; that where I am, there you may be also."*
> *John 14:2-4*

If you have trusted in Jesus as *your* Saviour, this includes you! You have a place reserved in the home of the Father, which is Heaven. Isn't this wonderful? There is a special reservation made for you! We can only imagine what that is like. But we can be certain of this: the Bridegroom is taking care of *your* future.

You can have absolute certainty that one day your new home will be in the *presence* of Jesus. It will be already prepared and it will be glorious! The space is plentiful. There are many rooms; Jesus was quite deliberate to make His disciples understand this fact, should they quarrel again over rights to the Kingdom.

Being in the presence of Jesus is simply enough; but what wonderful hope and comfort it is to know that those precious friends and loved ones in Christ will be in His presence too.

The disciples must have been greatly assured that this physical separation would not last. So too should we be encouraged. In fact, Jesus even said that if those who saw Him in the flesh and believed are blessed, how much more blessed are those that have not seen Him but have believed (John 20:29).

What a blessing it is to also know that our future is not only being prepared, it is also sealed and secure. 1 Peter 1:3-5 states:

"Blessed be the God and Father of our Lord Jesus Christ, who according to His abundant mercy has begotten us again to a living hope through the resurrection of Jesus Christ from the dead, to an inheritance incorruptible and undefiled and that does not fade away, reserved in heaven for you, who are kept by the power of God through faith for salvation ready to be revealed in the last time."

Spend a moment to consider this Scripture passage. I have a *living hope* because of the resurrection of Jesus Christ. He is the resurrection and the life (John 11:25). Just as Christ rose from the dead, I too will experience the power of His resurrection (Roman 6:4-5).

I have an inheritance that can't be corrupted, it can't be defiled, and it will never ever fade away. This triplet of characteristics about my inheritance reminds us of the permanence of God's promises.

It is an inheritance reserved for me. In other words, it has my name on it. And through faith, I am being kept by the power of God. Not by my own strength, not by my good works, not by my religious efforts, not by my own intelligence, but by the power of God. My eternal salvation is secured today because of His mercy, but it will be revealed in its fullest sense at a promised future time when I am in the presence of the Bridegroom.

The Bridegroom is getting ready

We have already considered that in the Jewish wedding, the bridegroom returns to his father's house. During the entirety of the betrothal period, the groom prepares his future marriage home where he will take his bride for the first night of their wedding. This would be located in his father's house.

It was important that the couple's new home was perfect for his bride. Only when it was ready could the bridegroom return and fetch his bride. However, there was one very important part of the process. Only the groom's father could determine when the new home was ready. This is a very important point: neither the bride nor the bridegroom could decide when the bridegroom returns.

So when we apply this to Christ and the Church, it reminds us that the Bridegroom is preparing a place for His Bride, the Church. But it is accompanied by two significant revelations.

Firstly, even though the Bride is to faithfully prepare for the coming of the Bridegroom, He is returning whether the Bride is ready or not.

This alone should challenge the Church to wake up out of complacency. We are mistaken if we think that the Bride is handling the wedding planner. We are even more in error if we have forgotten there is even a planned wedding at all!

Secondly, the return of Christ will not be ushered in by the Church preparing the perfect conditions here on earth. This doesn't negate the Church's special commission that must be undertaken until Christ's return, nor does it ignore the conditions and prophetic events that observant believers will recognise as characteristics of the End Times, but the decision for the Bridegroom returning to take His Bride rests firmly with God the Father.

In the Jewish tradition, there is only one person who decides when the bridegroom should return to get his betrothed bride and that is the father of the bridegroom. It is based solely on when the *place* being prepared for the bride by the bridegroom is ready.

That is the only prerequisite. It is *not* determined by whether the bride herself is ready

The wedding countdown is entirely in the Father's hands. John 14:1-4 explains that it will happen when the Son has *completed* preparation and only once the Father has *approved*. Therefore, *only* the Father knows when that day is.

According to Scripture, even the Bridegroom is uninformed about the time of His return, until instructed by the Father.

"But of that day and hour no one knows, not even the angels of heaven, but My Father only. But as the days of Noah were, so also will the coming of the Son of Man be."
Matthew 24:36-37

Look up

I can assure you that if the Son and the heavenly angels do not know the day and hour, neither does Satan! As we approach the return of the Bridegroom, spiritual forces of evil are projecting greater spiritual darkness that will trigger what the Bible terms as birth pangs (Matthew 24:8). This is an apt description, because like pain contractions during pregnancy, which incidentally were only introduced as a result of the Fall, end time events will escalate in intensity and frequency. As we approach the Lord's return, intervals between contractions will reduce and their severity will increase. I believe these birth pangs have begun. Let us be mindful, however, that the conclusion of the troubling birth pangs is one of joy for the Church and not sorrow.

And so it will be for the Christian, expectant of God's deliverance.

The Bible tells us in Luke 2:28:

"Now when these things begin to happen, look up and lift up your heads, because your redemption draws near."

So, we wait, we look up, we prepare. And we remember the Covenant that the Bridegroom made at 'His betrothal'. As we read in the previous chapter, the Bible tells us to remember the Lord's death *until* He returns. In fact, Scripture says that by doing this we "proclaim" it until He comes (1 Cor 11:26). For the Bridegroom's return is our living hope. This is our powerful deliverance. This is our great expectation.

> *I confess that Jesus Christ has risen from the dead. He is alive and He will return, just as He has promised. I know the Bridegroom is preparing a place for me in Heaven and for all those who love Him. I have an inheritance that is reserved in Heaven and it will not fade away. Thank you that it is being kept 'by the power of God through faith for salvation' that will one day be revealed to me in the Lord's time. Lord, You are my living hope. In these days in which we're living, please help me keep my eyes fixed on You. And I pray, "Come, Lord Jesus" (Rev 22:20).*

A bride at the Western Wall, Jerusalem, Israel

6

Preparation of the Bride

In the previous chapter we were reminded that the bridegroom would arrive to fetch the bride whether the bride is ready or not. This is why it was important for the bride to make herself ready.

It was Jewish custom, in an almost staged roleplay, for the bridegroom to come at a time that was unexpected, usually like a thief in the night, and 'snatch' his betrothed bride, who was patiently waiting for his return, and then take her to his prepared marital home.

The parable of the ten virgins in Matthew 25 has often been compared with this tradition. The bride would have young maidens (today better known as bridesmaids) who were to keep lamps ready at all times during the betrothal period in preparation for the bridegroom's arrival, so that when he came, they could lead the bridal procession to the home he had prepared for her. The bridegroom would be accompanied by his male friends who would blow a *shofar* (rams horn) to announce that the bridegroom had come to fetch his bride.

> *"And at midnight a cry was heard: 'Behold, the bridegroom is coming; go out to meet him!'*
> Matthew 25:6

Does this sound familiar? If it does, it's because the Bible tells us that there will be a day known only to the Heavenly Father when there will be a sounding of a trumpet (shofar) blast and a loud shout, and the Bride of Christ — all those who believe in Jesus Christ — will be snatched from this earth. They will be joined together with those believers in Christ who have already died, who will rise first. Thus, the Bride of Christ will meet with the Lord in the air to be with Him in the place prepared beforehand.

The fetching of the bride

In the English language, this event is known as 'the rapture' derived from the Latin word 'rapio', but in the original Greek it is translated 'caught up'.

1 Thessalonians 4:16-18 states,

For the Lord Himself will descend from heaven with a shout, with the voice of an archangel, and with the trumpet of God. And the dead in Christ will rise first. Then we who are alive and remain shall be caught up together with them in the clouds to meet the Lord in the air. And thus we shall always be with the Lord. Therefore comfort one another with these words.

This incredible event is the next milestone to occur in God's prophetic calendar. Nothing else is scheduled to happen before this event. It will mark the end of what is described as the 'Church Age' (the dispensation of Grace era in which Christ will build His Church) and usher in what is known as the Great Tribulation. The promise of the Bride being caught up, or snatched away, is indeed a reason to comfort one another. Firstly, because it means being united with the Bridegroom, and also because we will be rescued from the impending calamities of the Great Tribulation.

Although we don't know a date for when this will happen, Scripture warns us about the signs of the times that will precede this glorious event. These signs, or birth pangs as we contemplated earlier, should awaken the Church into readiness. Many of the signs are tribulations in their nature, but they are only a foretaste of the Great Tribulation that will occur after the Bride has been fetched (raptured).

Similarly, there are many antichrists during the present age (2 John 7:7), but it is a taster of *the* Antichrist who will be revealed during the Great Tribulation.

The signs that demonstrate we are nearing the Bridegroom's return should move us to be expectant, hopeful and prepared. It is my belief that we are living in the Last Days and experiencing these birth pangs more frequently. The day of the Bridegroom's trumpet blast is approaching.

We are at a time in God's prophetic calendar that we can describe as 'preparation of the Bride'. The Bridegroom is busy preparing a place for us, but what is the Bride doing?

To answer this question, let us return to the ancient Jewish wedding. There were many things that the bride would do to prepare for her groom, and we will look at each one and how they relate to the preparation of the Church.

Why prepare?

There are two misgivings that the Church might have in assuming readiness for the Bridegroom.

Firstly, it is incorrect to think that the Bride has to perfect the *earth* ready for Him to come. This isn't to be confused with the importance of the Church's mandate to do His work on earth and sow into the Kingdom here on earth – I will share the importance of this later in this book. However, the picture of the

Bridegroom coming to fetch His Bride clearly illustrates that *we* need to prepare to be *with Him.*

Imagine for a moment that you received a special invitation to meet the King. You decide to spend all your time getting your house ready, but not bothering to get changed yourself. You decide not to do your hair or wash, or prepare nice clothes. Your house is spotless, but you yourself are a mess. And then, after spending all your time on what you believed was important, you see on the invitation card that the venue was not your house, but the King's Palace. You realise that the only thing you had to do was the most important thing and that was to get yourself ready. How complicated you have made it. How regretful, that instead of being like Mary, you assumed the role of Martha. How foolish to not read the instructions that were key to being truly ready.

Now, please don't misunderstand me: the Bible says there *will be* a future time, separate to the Bride being fetched, that Christ will return to earth physically to reign. He will return to the Mount of Olives in Jerusalem in the same manner that He ascended. But on that Day, we, the Bride, will be returning *with Him.*

When this happens, it will be King Jesus who will put things straight as He comes to judge the earth in righteousness. Under His perfect rule, justice shall prevail. Therefore, we must prepare ourselves to be with Him in eternity. As Jesus told His disciples, "where I am, there you will be also," (John 14:3).

The second misgiving is made by those in the Church that have no interest in being ready or prepared at all! There are some sections of the Church that avoid mentioning the return of Christ in any way whatsoever.

In contrast, some might conclude that if it is all in the Lord's timing, why is there a need to prepare? After all, 'we have no control over His return, so let's not spend time speculating,' they might say.

But when Jesus spoke to His disciples about His Father's house having many rooms, He was preparing them for *life* without His physical presence. "Let not your heart be troubled," Jesus implored (John 14:1), before describing His Father's house. Jesus recognised the absence His death would create and what His followers would need to remain steadfast in their belief. At the same time, He was instilling in them a longing to be in His presence again, but this time in preparation to be with Him eternally. Jesus explained to His disciples that they will be with Him again one day, *but* this future was only guaranteed because they *knew the way (Verse 4).*

"And where I go you know, and the way you know."
John 14:4

Jesus elaborated on this, adding, "I am the way, the truth, and the life. No one comes to the Father except through Me," (Verse 6).

So here we begin to see how the invitation to be in Jesus's presence should compel us to choose the way, truth and life that Jesus is offering. Jesus also very clearly states that "no one comes to the Father except through me," and that those who know Jesus will also know the Father (Verse 7).

When the Bride fulfils its role of preparedness, the Church will adopt a much more Heaven-centred perspective. A Biblical world-view that includes being ready for the return of Jesus, will compel us to "observe the things above, not the things of the earth."

This perspective will help us develop a hunger to know the way, truth and life, and encounter a deeper relationship with the Father.

Set your mind on things above, not on things on the earth. For you died, and your life is hidden with Christ in God. When Christ who is our life appears, then you also will appear with Him in glory.
Colossians 3:2-4

So, to summarise, the Bride needs to be prepared for life in His presence. And by choosing the way, truth and life that Jesus has set out, we will desire a Heavenward mindset, an eternal perspective and a longing for His return. May this be the desire of the Church in these last days.

But God has not left the Bride to her own devices. The Bride doesn't wait for the Bridegroom without direction or purpose. The Bride has been given help.

Help in preparation

In the traditional Jewish wedding, the bride had some specific things to prepare. We will look at three key things that really resonated with me about the bride's preparation that has incredible parallels with how believers can live in preparation until the Bridegroom's return.

The Helper

In ancient Jewish custom, the father of the bridegroom would send a 'helper' to the bride's house during the period of the betrothal. The purpose of this helper was to teach her in the ways of the father's house (and by implication that of the son's).

This was important to the bride and the bridegroom because the bride's home wasn't going to be her home for much longer. Her future home was like that of her bridegroom's. In a society where there were different subcultures, it was important that preparation started during betrothal so that the bride could become accustomed for life forever with her groom.

If we return for a moment to Isaac and Rebekah's meeting, you will recall that Abraham sent his servant to choose a wife for Isaac. This servant's name was Eliezer, which means 'God's help', or 'God is my helper'. A part of Eliezer's commission by Abraham, sworn under oath, was to ensure that the suitable bride was accustomed to the culture and traditions of his master's house.

It is worth remembering that this earth is not going to be our home one day. Our Heavenly home awaits us. It is not like that of this world. The things of this world are remarkably different to the culture of the Father's Kingdom. Therefore, rather than waste time becoming more and more like the world we are in, let us spend time readying ourselves for God's Kingdom.

But we are not helpless in this endeavour. Our Heavenly Father has given us a Helper. The Bible says that this Helper is called the Holy Spirit.

The inception of the Church at Pentecost was brought about by the sending of the Holy Spirit, just as Jesus had promised His followers. Before His ascension into Heaven, Jesus had told His disciples to wait in Jerusalem for the Biblical feast of Shavuot. They waited for the Helper that Jesus had promised to comfort them in their separation. And on this important Jewish commemoration of the sending of the Law of Moses to convict His people of their sins, God used this powerful moment, 50 days after Jesus's resurrection, to release the Holy Spirit as the Helper that every follower of Christ would need in their lives.

The Bible says in John 14:26:

But the Helper, the Holy Spirit, whom the Father will send in My name, He will teach you all things, and bring to your remembrance all things that I said to you.

The Holy Spirit has various purposes, but one of these is to help believers become more like Christ and to *understand His ways*. The Holy Spirit 'teaches' and 'reminds' the Bride of the Bridegroom's words. Notice in this verse that the Holy Spirit is sent as a Helper on behalf of the Name of Jesus, just as the helper in ancient Jewish weddings would represent the bridegroom. Everything the Holy Spirit does points to Christ.

1 John 2:27b says,

> *...but as the same anointing teaches you concerning all things, and is true, and is not a lie, and just as it has taught you, you will abide in Him.*

Look carefully at the following verses in John 16 that explain that the Holy Spirit will lead Christ-followers *into all Truth.* And notice how the Holy Spirit will do so not in His own authority, but having received instruction *from the Father*. The Holy Spirit works inside the believer, bringing conviction about the things pleasing to the Father and the Son.

Notice also how the Holy Spirit has been commissioned to *tell us of things to come*, and how the Holy Spirit will take what is of the Son and declare it to His followers. In other words, it's the Holy Spirit that brings revelation into the spirit of the believer.

However, when He, the Spirit of truth, has come, He will guide you into all truth; for He will not speak on His own authority, but whatever He hears He will speak; and He will tell you things to come. He will glorify Me, for He will take of what is Mine and declare it to you. All things that the Father has are Mine. Therefore I said that He will take of Mine and declare it to you.
John 16:13-15

This is a striking picture of the Helper sent to the Bride by the Bridegroom's Father: comforting and guiding with full authority from the Father; revealing the ways of the Son and preparing for what is to come.

"All things that the Father has are Mine," verse 15 says. How remarkable it is that the Father has sent the Holy Spirit to help the Bride on earth as the Son and Father are working together.

Isn't it wonderful that the Holy Spirit teaches us not only how to live in our present home, but also for our eternal home that is being prepared for us. Our Helper is also reminding us of the promises of His Word that are life to us.

Another purpose of the Holy Spirit is to be our *comforter*. In fact, the word for 'helper' in John 14:26, which we read above ("But the Helper, the Holy Spirit, whom the Father will send in My name...") is the Greek word *parakletos*. This word also means 'comforter, consoler, advocate', and is translated 'Comforter' in some Bible translations.

The helper in the Jewish wedding custom would remind the bride of the bridegroom's love and affection during the period of separation. The helper would also comfort the bride and remind her of the bridegroom's promise to return. And in a similar way, the Holy Spirit is our comforter until the Bridegroom's return.

"Therefore comfort one another with these words," the Apostle Paul penned in 1 Thessalonians 4 after describing events of the rapture.

Jesus's return is the believer's hope and blessed assurance (Titus 2:13). Until this glorious day, the Christian can experience the revelation of the Son through the presence of the Holy Spirit. The betrothed believer now confesses that the life I now live, "I live by faith in the Son of God, who loved me and gave Himself for me," (Galatians 2:20).

Sending gifts

Sending gifts to one's fiancée might be one of the most common acts of a thoughtful bridegroom separated from his bride, so it should come as no surprise that in ancient Jewish custom the bridegroom would send gifts to his bride during the betrothal period. This was to help her remember him, to show his appreciation of her, and to provide a type of security that he would return to fetch her.

In the same manner, the Bride of Christ is in receipt of spiritual gifts to bless and sustain her until His return.

John 4:13 speaks about the permanence of our relationship with Him, which is sustained by the presence of the gift of the Holy Spirit:

By this we know that we abide in Him, and He in us, because He has given us of His Spirit.

Second Corinthians 1:21-22 speaks about the secure guarantee of our Salvation, which is sealed eternally by the Holy Spirit. It also says we have been anointed by the Holy Spirit – consecrated or set apart in Christ.

Now He who establishes us with you in Christ and has anointed us is God, who also has sealed us and given us the Spirit in our hearts as a guarantee.

Purity

Another important role of the Helper was to observe the Bride's purity during the betrothal. This is because at the *erusin* (betrothal) ceremony, also referred to as the *kiddushin* (sanctification), a covenant was made between the bride and bridegroom to keep themselves from impurity until their marital union. The bride vows to be 'consecrated' during the separation of the betrothal period, during which the bride was forbidden from being with another man until the bridegroom returns and takes his bride as his wife.

We only have to consider the betrothal of Mary and Joseph in the first advent to recognise the social stigma that would have been associated with Mary's unexpected pregnancy. Societal pressures would have even placed Mary in danger of being stoned like the adulterous woman in John 8, who was shown mercy by Jesus.

Whilst betrothal was as legally binding as marriage itself, Jewish law provided a means of divorce, called a *get*, that would allow the bridegroom to sever all ties to his bride in the event of her breaking her vow during their betrothal.

The Bible tells us that this is what Joseph had decided to do when he discovered that Mary was pregnant. But here we see the first glimpse of Joseph's true character: he was faithful to the Jewish law, but he also held a devotion to his bride. The Bible says that because he was a "just man", he didn't want Mary to be publicly shamed and maybe even worse, stoned for what he thought had happened. Understandably heartbroken, it says he decided to "put her away quietly" without public knowledge, by obtaining a *get*. This gave Joseph the right to legally divorce Mary under Jewish law and break off the betrothal, whilst protecting her from possible danger.

"Then Joseph her husband, being a just man, and not wanting to make her a public example, was minded to put her away secretly."
Matthew 1:19

We continue to read, however, that an angel of the Lord revealed to Joseph the miracle that had taken place:

"But while he thought about these things, behold, an angel of the Lord appeared to him in a dream, saying, "Joseph, son of David, do not be afraid to take to you Mary your wife, for that which is conceived in her is of the Holy Spirit."
Matthew 1:20

The news must have been received by Joseph with both relief and shock. When we consider the virgin birth, it makes sense that God chose a woman during the betrothal period. Mary wasn't chosen simply because she was a virgin, requiring God to do some urgent match-making to make sure she wasn't alone or embarrassed. Mary was chosen by God during the specific period in which she had consecrated herself to purity. The angel's confirmation gave assurance to Joseph, and to all who would hear of the virgin birth, that without doubt this was indeed a miraculous conception. But not only this, giving attention to a very human need, our compassionate and understanding Jehovah ensured by means of a covenant that a betrothed bridegroom was already in place to provide the earthly father that the Son of God would need.

We can conclude from these betrothal principles that faithfulness between bride and bridegroom was key to the bridegroom fulfilling the covenant and fetching his bride.

There is no question that the Bridegroom, Jesus, is faithful to the Church, but is the Church faithful to the Bridegroom?

Second Corinthians 11:2, warns,

"For I am jealous for you with godly jealousy. For I have betrothed you to one husband, that I may present you as a chaste virgin to Christ."

As we have previously noted, there is an important point to remember concerning the Bridegroom's return for His Bride: Jesus Christ is coming to gather the Church whether she is ready or not. This might challenge some of our preconceptions. Following the Jewish wedding blueprint, the bride's fetching is only ever determined by the bridegroom's father, irrespective of the bride's readiness. This doesn't negate the bride's need to be ready. In fact, it makes the bride's readiness even more necessary.

Therefore, the Church should commit to remain faithful to Jesus Christ. That includes fleeing the idolatry of our age and rejecting compromise with the world. The Church has been betrothed to "one husband", as it says in the Scripture above, in preparation for our union with Christ. It would be deceitful for the Church to have any other affection. As the Apostle John recorded the words of the Lord in Revelation 2 to the Church in Ephesus, "Nevertheless I have this against you, that you have left your first love."

Christ is not coming for an adulterous Bride. He is coming for a Bride that is faithful to Him. A Bride that is preserved blameless at the coming of our Lord Jesus Christ, as it says in 1 Thessalonians.

Now may the God of peace Himself sanctify you completely; and may your whole spirit, soul, and body be preserved blameless at the coming of our Lord Jesus Christ.
1 Thessalonians 5:23

We might be sceptical about whether the Church today is *worthy* to be received by the Bridegroom. But we should remember that it is the Holy Spirit that is cleansing and purifying the Church. The true Church – those mercifully saved by the power of God's forgiveness – is being washed and cleansed by the Word (Ephesians 5:26). It's important that the Church doesn't resist this process – the Helper is getting us ready for the return of the Bridegroom. If we abide in Him, "when He appears, we may have confidence and not be ashamed before Him at His coming," (1 John 2:28). It is God's will to present you 'blameless in the day of our Lord Jesus' (1 Corinthians 1:8).

God's love for the Church

In teaching about husbands and wives, the Apostle Paul made the following profound comparison:

Husbands, love your wives, just as Christ also loved the church and gave Himself for her, that He might sanctify and cleanse her with the washing of water by the word, that He might present her to Himself a glorious church, not having spot or wrinkle or any such thing, but that she should be holy and without blemish.
Ephesians 5:25

This great mystery, as Paul describes in verse 32, is speaking about Christ's love for the Church and how He laid down His life for her, illustrating how husbands should love their wives. In recent years we have witnessed an aggressive attempt to redefine the blueprint of Biblical marriage as union between a man and a woman. This shouldn't surprise us, because behind God's pattern for husband and wife, set out in Ephesians 5, is also the mystery behind the Bridegroom and the Church.

I believe that the Biblical definition of marriage is under attack not only because of the traditional Judeo-Christian values that it embodies, or because it was instituted by the Creator Himself, but also because spiritually it represents the 'DNA' behind Christ's relationship with His Church. Like all things that God considers Holy, it is a prime target for the enemy to undermine and destroy. The enemy seeks to distort the Biblical concept of marriage, just as he seeks to undermine Christ's relationship with the Church.

We read, "Just as Christ also loved the church and gave Himself for her." This comparison is foundational in comprehending the Good News of Jesus Christ and the marvellous, unparalleled love that our Saviour demonstrated for us on the Cross. The undermining of the Bible's definition of marriage, therefore, is simultaneously an indirect attack on this beautiful picture of the Gospel. In other words, twisting God's design for marriage between one man and one woman, and everything that it represents, is in direct conflict with a revelation of the Bride and Bridegroom and all the truths that we are discovering in this book.

It shouldn't surprise us, for Satan, who is the enemy of everything God has designed, is also an enemy of the Gospel. It is simply a vain attempt to eradicate the relationship between Christ and the people for whom He has saved out of darkness. But God's Word hasn't changed. He is coming back for a Bride that has forsaken the world and is consumed with the love of the Bridegroom.

In summary

Using the model of the bride's preparation during the betrothal period, we learn that the Church must prepare for Christ calling us home by applying the following:

1. Allowing the Holy Spirit, the Helper, to teach us the ways of the Father.
2. Remembering His covenant with us whilst awaiting His return.
3. Not forgetting our first love by keeping away from idolatry.

I am part of the Bride, the Church of Jesus Christ, Who loves the Church and gave Himself for her. I pray that the Church will seek after all truth and reject all forms of compromise. Thank You, Father, for the gift of the Holy Spirit who is working in my life and will continue sanctifying me for His purpose. I invite your Spirit to prepare me for eternity, but also to prepare me for today. I abide in You through Your Spirit. You are my Comforter, You are my Helper, You are my Advocate, and I need You in my life. You are my first love; please teach me Lord to know all your ways and may Your Spirit lead me according to Your perfect will.

7

The Bride is ready

We have considered the covenant that is made to commence the betrothal period. We have looked at the preparation by the bridegroom and separate preparation by the bride. Now, we come to the bridegroom fetching the bride and taking her to be with him forever.

Bible times

When the bridegroom fetches his bride, he comes to take her from her family home to his father's house. As illustrated by several Old Testament examples, it is at this point that the marriage is consummated. It was tradition that the couple would spend a period of time in one another's company. After this period, the bridegroom would present his bride at the wedding feast (*seudah*), a joyous occasion attended by family and friends as guests. This feast of food, dancing and celebration could have even lasted for several days. This sequence is significant when understanding what lies ahead for Christ and the Church. We will return to this thought shortly, but firstly I would like to share how this ancient tradition translates in the modern day.

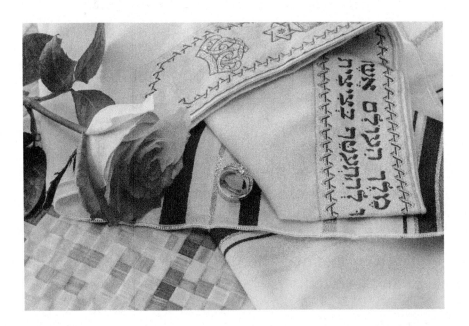

Today

Today, the Jewish wedding takes parts of the ancient Jewish tradition of Bible times and condenses them. Join me now as we accept the invitation to attend a typical traditional Jewish wedding.

First part

Even before the wedding day, two separate receptions are held (usually in adjacent rooms) – one is for the bride and another for the bridegroom. It is tradition that the bride and groom refrain from seeing one other for a full week prior to their wedding, so that their love and yearning for each other is increased, and that they experience heightened joy at being reunited at their wedding.

The bride is sitting on an ornate throne-like chair. Her close friends and family approach her and wish *Mazal Tov* and other personal words of encouragement, in a similar way to how Rebekah received a special blessing by her family before leaving to be united with Isaac. How wonderful that this reference to Israel's past is incorporated.

Meanwhile, at the groom's reception, songs are being sung and the Torah is recited in joyful anticipation.

As is the custom with many families, they are now signing the *ketubah*, the marriage contract, that specifies the bridegroom's commitments to the bride. It will be signed by two appointed Jewish witnesses. This family has decided to create a beautiful artwork for the *ketubah* that will be framed and displayed in a special place in the married couple's new home. You might recognise that this is the covenant-making ceremony that preceded the betrothal in ancient Israel.

Now that these receptions and the *ketubah* signings are complete, the wedding will continue with the *badeken,* a veiling ceremony. A procession, led by the bridegroom, enters the bridal reception room and the groom covers the bride's face with a veil. Again, it points us back to the story of Rebekah, when she veiled her face when meeting her bridegroom, Isaac. The veil emphasises the importance that the bridegroom's interests should not be solely on the bride's external appearance, but rather her inner beauty, and symbolises the innate modesty that the bride possesses.

Now that the bridegroom has veiled his bride, the parents of the bride and groom approach the bride and bless her.

After the *badeken,* we watch the couple enter the main ceremony, where we are seated with all the guests. This is in fact the holiest day of this couple's life and the ceremony reflects this.

Our attention turns to an ornate canopy on four poles, known as the *chuppah*. This is the main focal point of the ceremony and represents the new home that the bride and groom will create following their marriage. The couple enter the canopy together, escorted by their respective parents. The sides of the canopy are open on all sides, representing the commitment to establish a home that will always be open to guests, as was the tent of Abraham and Sarah.

This couple has decided, like many do, to follow the custom of holding the chuppah beneath the open skies. It's such a beautiful night. You can see thousands upon thousands of stars above us, and it feels like they are twinkling with even more intensity tonight for this special couple. This custom of open skies above the chuppah recalls God's covenant blessing to Abraham, promising that his descendants will be as numerous as the stars.

It also symbolises the couple's resolve to establish a household that will reside under the Sovereignty of Almighty God, Creator of Heaven and Earth. It's as if the same audience of stars that witnessed Isaac's first meeting with Rebekah, and millions of couples since, are once again on display to remind us of this precious covenant. Such is the awe and magnitude of this spiritual significance, many brides and bridegrooms are moved to tears, aware of the solemnity of this moment. And so it is with our couple. It's hard not to be moved to tears as well, and we're just the guests!

Here is perhaps an explanation why. It is believed that the Shekinah, the glory of God's divine presence, graces every chuppah ceremony. What a privilege it is to witness this occasion in the presence of the Almighty.

In most Jewish communities, the bride and groom will have fasted prior to the wedding to prepare for entering God's presence under the chuppah. The purity of the bride is symbolised by her white dress, and likewise the purity of the bridegroom is symbolised by his pristine white *kittel,* a long white frock traditionally worn on Yom Kippur.

Another symbolism of purity is through a tradition called *mikvah,* which takes place before the wedding. This is a running bath in which Jewish brides immerse themselves. This joyous occasion is usually celebrated by a small party of the bride's female friends during which the women gift scented soaps and perfumes. Perhaps this was a precursor to the all-female parties that are popular today in celebration of the bride prior to most contemporary weddings.

Back to the ceremony. the proceedings under the chuppah involve some thought-provoking customs with meaningful expression.

We witness the couple escorted to the chuppah with an entourage of family members, each holding a candle, reminiscent of the maidens carrying lamps in Matthew 25. The candle represents the flickering light and fire that occurred at the giving of the Torah, which is described in Judaism as the marriage of God and Israel under the "chuppah" of Mount Sinai. In fact, Isaiah 62 describes the joy of the Lord at Zion's salvation, "And as the bridegroom rejoices over the bride, so shall your God rejoice over you," (Isaiah 62:5b).

The couple enter like king and queen; this royal-like treatment is intentionally planned to honour this special procession. This couple have chosen their respective married parents to serve as their 'honour guards', as is the usual custom, but they have also included their grandparents in the entourage like many couples choose to do as well.

With the band playing a moving melody, the bridegroom is led into the chuppah first and then the bride. The order is significant. Her arrival second to the bridegroom reaffirms the bride's consent to be married to the man under the chuppah, but also is symbolic of the groom inviting his bride to join him in his domain, where he receives her gladly.

Before she enters, this bride is keeping a tradition of circling the bridegroom seven times – seven is a significant number in Judaism, symbolising completeness and wholeness, something accomplished through the marriage union.

Some brides circle three times to represent the three expressions of betrothal between God and Israel in the book of Hosea 2:19-20:

"I will **betroth** you to Me forever [Circle 1]

Yes, I will **betroth** you to Me
In righteousness and justice,
In lovingkindness and mercy; [Circle 2]

I will betroth you to Me in faithfulness, [Circle 3]
And you shall know the Lord."

As the bride enters the chuppah a cantor is singing a hymn in Hebrew. The words are calling upon God to bless the bride and groom, and if a parent is deceased it would bring acknowledgement to their memory.

Based on the Torah, the marriage is a two-staged process in which two cups of wine are used.

The first stage, as we have already covered, is called the *erusin* (meaning betrothal), which is also referred to as *kiddushin,* which means 'sanctified or dedicated'. The first cup is raised by the rabbi who blesses the wine and then recites the betrothal blessing. Once the blessing is recited, the bride and bridegroom drink from the cup, dedicating their marriage to God.

In Jewish law, the marriage only becomes official legally once the bridegroom gives an object of value to the bride, and like many Jewish grooms, this bridegroom gives his bride a ring. The circular characteristic of the ring depicts the marriage covenant. The ring is usually plain as it is hoped the marriage will be one of simple beauty. As the bridegroom places the ring on his bride's finger, he says, "With this ring, you are consecrated to me according to the law of Moses and Israel."

Now that the ring has been placed

on the bride's finger, the aforementioned *ketubah* (the marriage contract) is read aloud in original Aramaic text and given to the bridegroom for him to present to his bride. The ketubah details the bridegroom's promises to provide for his bride and becomes the property of the bride, who is to keep it safe for all the days of their marriage.

Some Jews compare the ketubah document with when Moses read the Torah to the Jews at Mount Sinai. And you can see why. The God of Israel has promised to provide for the needs of His people.

Second part

The ketubah presentation serves as a division between the two stages under the chuppah. The second stage is called the *nissuin*, which in Hebrew means 'to take' and derives from the word *naso*, which means 'to lift up'. The nissuin involves the recitation of the Seven Blessings (known as *Sheva Brachot*). These blessings are recited over the second cup of wine. As it takes place, family and close friends are honoured to approach the chuppah.

The first three of these ancient blessings are as follows: a blessing over the wine as a symbol of joy; a blessing praising God to whom all creation proclaims praise; a blessing praising God as Creator of humanity, and the fourth blessing praises God Who created humanity in the Divine image.

The fifth blessing is the hope for the Messiah. The sixth blessing is a prayer for the happiness of the bride and groom. The seventh and final blessing combines the individual hope for the couple's happiness with a prayer for joy in the Messianic future. Once these seven ancient blessings are said, the couple share the second cup of wine. It is believed that at this point the bride and groom become 'one'.

Suddenly, a cup is placed in a napkin at the foot of the bridegroom who stamps on it, shattering the glass into two pieces. This signals the start of the party with cheering, dancing and shouts of "Mazal Tov".

There are several thoughts behind the glass smashing. One symbolism is the reminder that despite the height of personal joy, Jews must not forget the destruction of the Temple and city of Jerusalem 2,000 years ago, and should yearn for the Jewish people's return there. Another picture is the hope that the couple's children will be as numerous as the shards of glass.

Shouts of "Mazal Tov!" have erupted. The now-married couple depart the main ceremony and we must wait patiently for their return to the celebration.

The final part of the service, called the *Yichud*, has now begun, but we are not present.

Yichud comes from the word 'yachad', which translates "together" in Hebrew, and is considered one the most intimate and private parts of the day. The bride and groom are required to spend time alone away from family and guests to reflect on the magnitude of the special moment that just took place – their marriage – before joining the celebrations with wedding guests.

Remember that in ancient Israel this time alone is when the marriage would have been consummated, after which the bridegroom would present his bride to the jubilant guests waiting in anticipation at the wedding feast. Today, yichud is not used to physically consummate the marriage, but in its honour, couples in the contemporary Jewish wedding spend a short time alone privately before returning to their guests. In religious circles, it is the first opportunity for the couple to have physical contact now that they are married, and the ritual varies within Jewish communities.

Inside the room, aptly called 'the yachud room', it is customary for the bride to bless the groom. She says, "May you merit to have a long life, and to unite with me in love from now until eternity. May I merit to dwell with you forever."

Also inside the room, the couple traditionally breaks their wedding day fast. The bride and groom usually exchange gifts. The newly-weds will often eat, talk and relax together before entering the party. Even in some contemporary Christian weddings, the couple will spend some time together privately between the church ceremony and the wedding reception, perhaps originating from this Jewish tradition.

Third part

When the bride and groom emerge from the yichud room to join their guests, they are ceremoniously greeted with music, singing and dancing. We must prepare ourselves: everyone is expected to join the dancing! The men dance with the groom, and the women with the bride, traditionally in separate circles. Once the first dance is completed, the couple, their family and the rabbi sit at the head table, and the wedding meal (*Seudah Mitzvah*) commences. Interestingly, the wedding meal is a requirement by Jewish law.

After the meal, the 'Grace after Meals' is said as well as the Sheva Brachot, the same seven blessings that were recited underneath the chuppah. Again, two full cups of wine are prepared for the blessings. It's as if the spiritual significance of the cup of wine and the wedding are inseparable, from beginning to end.

This time six of the wedding guests are invited to recite the first six blessings of the Sheva Brachot. The wine in the two cups are then blended and the groom sips from one cup and the bride from the other.

This beautiful event now comes to a close, but the special union has only just begun.

The parallels

Now that we have covered all of the components of the traditional Jewish wedding, we can now align the Hebrew names of the various stages of the wedding to the parts I outlined earlier in the book.

First stage
Erusin (Betrothal ceremony)
also known as **Kiddushin** (Dedication)
and includes **Ketubah** (The Covenant)

The Separation (Betrothal)
The Preparation of the Bride
The Preparation of the Bridegroom

Second stage
Nissuin (Bridegroom fetches the Bride)
Yichud (The consummation of the marriage)

Third stage
Seudah Mitzvah (The wedding feast)

The union

There are no words that can adequately describe the incredible joy at the Bride being united with the Bridegroom. Keep in mind the elements of the ancient Jewish wedding:

The **betrothal**, instituted by the cup of covenant.

The **separation**, in which the bridegroom departs, but promises to return.

The **purifying** *mikvah*, in which the bride 'makes herself ready' just before the wedding.

The bridegroom **'fetching'** the bride.

The couple **entering the home** of the bridegroom's father.

The period of time when the bridegroom and bride are **alone privately** without guests.

Then the joyous occasion when the bridegroom 'presents his bride' to the wedding guests and the **celebratory feast** that takes place for seven days.

All of these elements hold wonderful truths, and we will now continue to discover them more closely.

Dressed and ready

After the Bridegroom has 'fetched' His Bride, the Church, we will be in the presence of Jesus Christ in the place He has prepared for us. Every person throughout history that has put their trust in Jesus Christ will be present. Because of Jesus's atoning sacrifice, the Church will be presented blameless and  a wedding feast will subsequently take place.

We can be confident of our attendance if we have invited Him into our lives, because the Bible says that just as Christ defeated death by rising from the dead, so too will we be resurrected from the dead and receive eternal life.

But now Christ is risen from the dead, and has become the firstfruits of those who have fallen asleep. For since by man came death, by Man also came the resurrection of the dead. For as in Adam all die, even so in Christ all shall be made alive.
2 Corinthians 15:20-22

Revelation 19 portrays a beautiful picture of the union that will be established. Notice the vocabulary has now changed. No longer do we read the term 'bride', but rather 'wife' (verse 7). For amid this great celebration is the realisation that God's purpose is finally accomplished.

The sense of this accomplishment is amplified by the reminder at the start of Revelation 19 that speaks of a "great harlot who corrupted the earth with her fornication," (verse 2). This 'great harlot' is not part of the true Church that has entered into God's eternal promise. The world system set up under Satan's directive, a system that was responsible for the persecution of believers, is now subject to God's righteous judgement and eternal wrath.

It's helpful to be reminded of this contrast. Our union with Christ is not just an automatic right, it is a victorious deliverance from what would otherwise have been our destined future. This is the expression of His deep love for us. It is a union that we did not deserve because of sin, had it not been for His great mercy and grace. John 3:16 tells us, "For God so loved the world that He gave His only begotten Son, that whoever believes in Him should not perish but have everlasting life."

The Bride is rescued from the corruption that ensues on earth under Satan's authority until the Lord God Almighty puts all of Christ's enemies under Jesus's feet.

"Alleluia! Salvation and glory and honour and power belong to the Lord our God! For true and righteous are His judgments, because He has judged the great harlot who corrupted the earth with her fornication; and He has avenged on her the blood of His servants shed by her."
Revelation 19:2

In stark contrast to God's wrath directed at the great harlot, we then read about the marriage of the Lamb that is met with great rejoicing.

"Let us be glad and rejoice and give Him glory, for the marriage of the Lamb has come, and His wife has made herself ready." And to her it was granted to be arrayed in fine linen, clean and bright, for the fine linen is the righteous acts of the saints.
Revelation 19:7-8

Let us be in no doubt, this wedding 'dress' as depicted in Revelation 19 is 'granted' to the Church. It is given to us.

The word translated 'fine linen' is *byssinos*. The word is used to refer to the fine linen used to clothe Joseph when he was appointed as a leader in Egypt. It was also used to make the tabernacle. It was used in parts of Aaron's priestly robe as well as for King David's robe.

Can you see the common theme here? *Byssinos* suggests a robe that is both royal and priestly. After all, the marriage supper of the Lamb is the commencement of the believer's eternal reward in reigning with Christ. Yes, that is right, the Bible says we shall share in His throne and His authority as kings and priests.

Let's take a look at some passages in Revelation that confirm this.

To him who overcomes I will grant to sit with Me on My throne, as I also overcame and sat down with My Father on His throne.
Revelation 3:21

To Him who loved us and washed us from our sins in His own blood, and has made us kings and priests to His God and Father, to Him be glory and dominion forever and ever. Amen.
Revelation 1:5b-6

For You were slain,
And have redeemed us to God by Your blood
Out of every tribe and tongue and people and nation,

*And have made us kings and priests to our God;
And we shall reign on the earth."*
Revelation 5:9b-10

These Scriptures reaffirm that we will have a future role in the kingly and priestly one thousand year reign of Christ on the earth. But they also show *why* such privilege is granted to us.

They are granted because of the cleansing blood of Jesus! No wonder these robes will be 'clean and white'! Remember, the Bride will have completed a process of purification that every individual believer will go through at the judgement seat of Christ. This can be likened to the bridal *mikvah* that must take place just before the wedding.

In the case of the believer, it will be where each person "will give an account of himself to God," (Romans 14:12) and it will take place after the rapture, but *before* the wedding feast. This is not the same as the final judgement of the wicked. It is not a judgement that determines salvation – this is secure and certain for the believer in Christ. Rather it is the judgement where believers will receive what is due for the things done while on earth.

The "fine linen, clean and bright" will be for the "righteous acts of the saints" (Revelation 19:7-8). The term 'saints' refers to believers in Jesus Christ. Whilst the blood of Jesus is enough to be granted our participation in the marriage supper of the Lamb, the "acts of the saints" will largely determine the adorning of the Bride's garment of fine linen. In other words, the righteous acts of believers whilst on earth matter to God. They have eternal significance because they will one day be brought to light at the judgement seat of Christ. They will be metaphorically woven into the robe of the wife of the Lamb, adorning her in readiness for this spectacular, joyful occasion.

This we can be certain of: we, the Church, will be purified and perfected because of the cleansing work of Jesus Christ. The Church should give attention to its purity today, but its perfection will be complete in the fullest sense on that Day when we will enter into union with Christ.

Lord, thank you that I am loved by You. You have promised me eternal life, a future and a hope. I live to see Jesus work in my life and among my friends and family today. And I long to bring my loved ones into Your Kingdom and whoever you put before my path. May 'your kingdom come and your will be done on earth as it is in heaven'. This is my temporary home, but one day I will be in the presence of Jesus. There, I will be given a new perfected body and will be cleansed ready to reign with Christ. May the things I do on this earth be glorifying to You. In your mercy, may they be woven into the fine linen of the Bride's gown.

8

Feast, Friends & Future

We have already considered how the Jewish wedding provides a framework for understanding the Bridegroom's fetching of the Bride. Before continuing, let's review some key principles that this Jewish wedding picture, in harmony with Scripture, shows us.

Reviewing the principles

Right now, the Church is living in the first phase of the wedding, the 'betrothal period'. This 'betrothal period' is happening now in the present Church Age as people, both Jew and Gentile, put their trust in Jesus Christ as personal Saviour. The Church is betrothed to Christ by the New Covenant, but is separated physically as the Bridegroom prepares a place in His Father's house.

The second phase is the bridegroom taking the bride from her house to his father's house. This will be fulfilled when Christ takes His Bride, the true Church, from this world to His Father's house in Heaven in an event known as 'the rapture'. This will gather both Christian believers living at the time and those believers who have already died.

The Marriage and the Marriage Supper of the Lamb are two separate events, despite sounding similar. The Marriage can be compared to the ancient Jewish tradition when the bride and bridegroom enter physical union at the father's house. This is a period set aside exclusively for Christ and the Church. It will not be in the home of the Bride (on the earth), but rather in Heaven after the Bride has been fetched. Therefore, it will be *after* the rapture and the judgement seat of Christ. And no guests will be present.

The Marriage Supper of the Lamb (also known as the Marriage Feast), however, is the celebration that immediately *follows* the Marriage. In the Jewish wedding, you will recall that the bridegroom returns with the bride to participate in the much-anticipated wedding feast, where they are joined by guests already assembled. This is not simply a party to celebrate the couple, nor is it only tradition. Rather, it is an essential component of the wedding that is mandated by Jewish law. This illustrates the importance of the wedding feast, and why the Marriage Supper of the Lamb must definitely take place for this Biblical wedding analogy to be fully complete.

We have already established that the Marriage Feast must happen after the rapture *and* after the Marriage itself, but there are differing views, all still in agreement with the dispensationalist view, that query its actual location.

Some Bible theologians believe that it will take place in Heaven *before* Christ returns with the Church to earth to set up His Millennial reign, whilst others believe it will take place *after* Christ's return, at the start of Christ's Millennial reign on earth.

The latter is certainly consistent with the picture of the Bridegroom and Bride 'returning' together after the marriage to a feast that will include guests (I will describe the guests shortly). There are also a number of parables that associate a wedding feast taking place in God's Kingdom, which if aligned with Christ's Millennial Kingdom reign on earth, would also support the view that the Marriage Supper of the Lamb takes place upon Christ's Second Coming.

However, those who believe that the Marriage Supper of the Lamb takes place in Heaven before Christ's Second Coming contend that the nature of Christ's return to earth to execute judgement and cast the Antichrist into the Lake of Fire does not reflect the joyful, celebratory occasion typically associated with a wedding feast, which is more suited to Heaven. The Second Coming of Jesus depicts a different kind of picture of Christ, who returns on a white horse as conquering Messiah, with the hosts of Heaven at his side, setting foot on the Mount of Olives in Jerusalem to set up His Millennial Kingdom on earth. On his robe and on his thigh He has written: "King of Kings and Lord of Lords."

Also, the ancient Jewish wedding tradition of holding the marriage feast at the groom's father's home fits with the understanding that the Marriage Supper of the Lamb will take place in Heaven and its length of time (typically seven days), would fit the picture that the Tribulation lasts for seven years.

The important thing to remember is that one Messiah, Jesus Christ, fulfils different roles depending on the era of dispensation, without conflicting His character or Sonship. For example, Jesus's first coming as suffering Messiah is the same Jesus whose second coming will be as conquering Messiah. But the differentiating characteristics help us understand God's purpose for the era, His Sovereign plan, and how we relate to it.

My personal conclusion is that the Marriage Feast takes place in Heaven, but the purpose of this book isn't to argue either view. However, what we should be convinced about is that the Marriage Supper of the Lamb *will* take place and will be an event of great joy. We can also be certain that Christ will return to earth to judge the world and set up His Millennium Kingdom. When Christ returns to earth, it will be *with* His Church and the hosts of Heaven, and we will reign with Him.

The most important thing as human beings needing a Saviour, is to be certain in our hearts that we will be present. And we can be assured of this through faith in Jesus Christ. The rest will unfold to our wonder and joy.

Blessed and holy is he who has part in the first resurrection. Over such the second death has no power, but they shall be priests of God and of Christ, and shall reign with Him a thousand years.
Revelation 20:6

Friends of the Bridegroom

Have you ever heard of a wedding feast where the bride and bridegroom are the only ones in attendance? Such an arrangement couldn't really be described as a 'feast' without guests. Even small intimate weddings usually have a number of wedding guests in attendance at least.

So, who else will be in attendance at the Marriage Supper of the Lamb? Revelation 19:9 says, "Blessed are those who are called to the marriage supper of the Lamb!" This suggests that there are some in attendance that are not categorised as the 'Bride'.

The Bible speaks about friends of the Bridegroom that will already be assembled. Whilst God is Sovereign and knows who will be in attendance, I believe the Bible gives us a clue that those in attendance at the Marriage Feast, in addition to the Bride, are those that preceded the Church before

Pentecost, but had a relationship with the God of Abraham, Isaac and Jacob.

For example, John the Baptist described himself as 'the friend of the bridegroom'.

John 3:29 states:

He who has the bride is the bridegroom; but the friend of the bridegroom, who stands and hears him, rejoices greatly because of the bridegroom's voice. Therefore this joy of mine is fulfilled.

This wonderful explanation by John the Baptist carries even deeper meaning. He wasn't just 'a friend' but '*the* friend' of the Bridegroom. He was actually describing himself as what we refer today as the best man. It was Jewish custom for the 'best man' to ask the bridegroom whether he loved the bride, and when hearing the groom's declaration, he would shout with jubilation. This is what John the Baptist did when he heard the voice of Jesus: "Behold! The Lamb of God who takes away the sin of the world!" (John 1:29) and in John 3:29, "the friend of the bridegroom, who stands and hears him, rejoices greatly because of the bridegroom's voice. Therefore this joy of mine is fulfilled."

In this sense, John the Baptist was a forerunner in preparation for Christ as the Bridegroom. He prepared the way for Jesus, much like the tradition of the Jewish friends of the bridegroom who announced the groom's coming. We see this depicted in Matthew

25 in the Parable of the Wise and Foolish Virgins. It says in verse 6, "And at midnight a cry was heard: 'Behold, the bridegroom is coming; go out to meet him!'". It was tradition for the male friends of the bridegroom to carry out the message of the groom's coming in advance of his arrival.

Jesus also referred to His disciples as 'friends of the bridegroom', a description He used for them *whilst* He was with them. Mark 2:19-20 states: "And Jesus said to them, 'Can the friends of the bridegroom fast while the bridegroom is with them? As long as they have the bridegroom with them they cannot fast. But the days will come when the bridegroom will be taken away from them, and then they will fast in those days.'"

There is also an incredible event told to us in the Gospels where important Biblical figures accompanied Jesus in the most amazing scene. We read about 'the transfiguration' in Matthew 17, where Jesus took Peter, James and John up a mountain and Moses and Elijah appeared with Jesus. It has been pointed out that Moses was present as he represented the Law and Elijah represented the Prophets. The Bible even mentions that they spoke about Jesus's death "which He was about to accomplish".

It's quite profound when we consider that right here in the New Testament, Jesus had dialogue with two of the most important Old Testament figures: Moses and Elijah. These two Jewish forerunners were sent by the Father as a type of friend of the

Bridegroom, to prepare the Son for His divine appointment at the Cross.

This incredible event was concluded with the voice of the Father: "This is My beloved Son, Hear Him." Compare this with the Father's declaration after the aforementioned friend of the Bridegroom, John the Baptist, had immersed Jesus in the River Jordan: "This is My beloved Son, in whom I am well pleased," (Matthew 3:17). All these friends had an important role on behalf of God the Father in preparing for the fulfilment of the Bridegroom's mission.

We can also confidently deduce the following. If Moses and Elijah were in the presence of Jesus then, there is no reason to doubt that they are in Jesus's presence today.

John the Baptist, Moses and Elijah were three of many forerunners that prepared the way for the Messiah. God chose the lineage of Abraham, Isaac, Jacob and their descendants and gave them an everlasting covenant in preparation for the arrival of a Jewish Messiah. Their testimonies are recorded in Hebrews 11 along with David, Rahab, Samuel and other named and unnamed Bible heroes of faith, who overcame unbelievable challenges and hardships as they strived to attain 'the Promise'.

Hebrews 11:39-40 says,

And all these, having obtained a good testimony through faith, did not receive the promise, God having provided something better for us, that they should not be made perfect apart from us.

Then, at the beginning of the next chapter (Hebrews 12), it begins, "Therefore we also, since we are surrounded by so great a cloud of witnesses..." This phrase 'cloud of witnesses' is directly linked to the list of names in Hebrews 11 and all those 'too many to mention' (Hebrews 11:32).

The original Greek phrase for 'cloud of witnesses' refers to the very top rows of the Greek athletics stadium from which spectators would view the race. It became known as 'the clouds'. In their witness 'from above', even if only metaphorical, the faithful, overcoming witnesses of Hebrews 11 are observers of the One who has run the race, the "author and finisher of our faith, who for the joy that was set before Him endured the Cross, despised the shame, and has sat down at the right hand of the throne of God," (Hebrews 12:2). Their inclusion in the Marriage Supper of the Lamb doesn't exclude the centrality of the Cross; in fact, it points us towards it. It is as if this cloud of witnesses was given special observing status of what took place at Calvary.

Remember, Hebrews 11 says the Old Testament overcomers didn't receive the promise, but rather it was fulfilled through Jesus Christ. It was as if Jesus's sacrifice on the Cross was the *end fulfilment* of the faith of these Old Testament heroes in the same way that it is the *beginning of the faith* of every overcoming believer since.

Perhaps this casts new light on the phrase, "Jesus, the author and finisher" of our faith. He is the author of our faith as New Covenant believers and He is the finisher of the faith of these 'friends of the Bridegroom'.

Christ's victory on the Cross was a defining moment for all mankind, and is why this 'cloud of witnesses' will also be in attendance at the Marriage Supper of the Lamb. As the Bride of Christ, we shall enjoy the company of these heroes of faith.

Tribulation saints

To avoid any unintended omission, it must be mentioned that we can have full confidence that those who come to Christ during the Great Tribulation (after the Church has been raptured), will also reign with Christ in the millennium. Even though the earth will be subject to unprecedented turmoil, which the Bride has been rescued from, those that turn to Christ during this Tribulation period will experience God's saving grace. Don't wait until then, however, to receive Jesus if you have not done so already.

In the book of Revelation, John sees a large number of these tribulation saints (believers) who have been martyred by the Antichrist.

After these things I looked, and behold, a great multitude which no one could number, of all nations, tribes, peoples, and tongues, standing

*before the throne and before the Lamb, clothed
with white robes, with palm branches in their
hands, and crying out with a loud voice, saying,
"Salvation belongs to our God who sits on the
throne, and to the Lamb!*
Revelation 7:9-10

When John asks who they are, he is told, "These
are the ones who come out of the great tribulation,
and washed their robes and made them white in the
blood of the Lamb," (Verse 14).

Even though tribulation saints will be living in
the midst of great persecution, they will be faithful to
the end, even to the point of death:

*And they overcame him by the blood of the Lamb
and by the word of their testimony, and they did
not love their lives to the death.*
Revelation 12:11

Israel restored

There is another feast mentioned in the Bible that
is separate to the Marriage Supper of the Lamb. This
second feast is foreshadowed by what the Bible
describes as 'Feast of Tabernacles'. Yes, the Feast of
Tabernacles will take place in Christ's Millennial
reign on earth, upon His physical return. It will
include the redeemed remnant of Israel, together
with the nations of the earth. Every knee will bow

and every tongue will confess Jesus as King, who will reign from David's throne in Jerusalem.

The Bible says that God has not forsaken Israel despite their collective rejection of Jesus as Messiah at His first coming. Isaiah prophesied that a faithful 'remnant' of Israel would one day "be called the Holy People, the Redeemed of the LORD," (Isaiah 62:12).

The Bible shows that the Jewish nation's spiritual blindness during the Church Age is both temporary and partial.

Romans 11:25 says,

"...that blindness in part has happened to Israel until the fullness of the Gentiles has come in."

The blindness is *temporal* because it will last until God determines; it's *partial* because, as illustrated by Paul's testimony, the first Apostles (who were all Jewish), the early Church (comprised largely of Jews) and every Jewish person who has since accepted Christ, salvation is "for the Jew first and also for the Greek," (Romans 1:16).

However, Israel's collective rejection of Jesus Christ was prophesied in the Old Testament: "He is despised and rejected by men," (Isaiah 53:3a). But the heart of God has continued to long for Israel's restoration. Acts 2:36 says,

"Therefore let all the house of Israel know assuredly that God has made this Jesus, whom you crucified, both Lord and Christ."

Although there is a veil in place upon the nation of Israel today, Christ the Bridegroom is key to the veil being lifted.

> *But their minds were blinded. For until this day the same veil remains unlifted in the reading of the Old Testament, because the veil is taken away in Christ. But even to this day, when Moses is read, a veil lies on their heart. Nevertheless **when one turns to the Lord**, the veil is taken away.*
> 2 Corinthians 3:14-16

"When one turns to the Lord, the veil is taken away." Although there is a unique veiling of Israel's eyes, it is also worth pointing out that any person who is in unbelief has a type of veil before their eyes that needs lifting. And when that person turns to the Lord, the veil is lifted.

> *"But we all, with unveiled face, beholding as in a mirror the glory of the Lord, are being transformed into the same image from glory to glory, just as by the Spirit of the Lord."*
> 2 Corinthians 3:18

Israel's rejection is not final

For a proper perspective of Israel's restoration, in Romans 11 the Apostle Paul describes a number of important principles for Gentiles to understand regarding Israel's collective rejection of Christ.

1. Through their "fall", salvation has come to the Gentiles (v11). Through their "disobedience", "He might have mercy on all" (v32).
2. If their "failure" brought spiritual "riches" for the Gentiles, "how much more [will] their fulness [be]" (v12). How much will their "acceptance be" but "life from the dead?" (v15).
3. The natural branches (Israel) were broken off due to unbelief, so that the Gentiles can be "grafted in" (v19).
4. Gentiles shouldn't "boast" against the branches because the "root supports you" (v18).
5. God is able to "graft them in again" to their "own olive tree" (v23-24).
6. They are "beloved for the sake of the father. For the gifts and the calling of God are irrevocable" (v28-29).

To summarise, Israel's rejection of Christ as Messiah is in part and for a period; it has allowed the Gentiles to be grafted into God's plan for Salvation; God has not forsaken Israel, but will graft them in again. One day, in accordance with His Word, the collective scales will fall from Israel's eyes and the most amazing revelation will take place.

Zechariah 12:10 states,

"And I will pour on the house of David and on the inhabitants of Jerusalem the Spirit of grace and supplication; then they will look on Me whom they pierced..."

This spiritual restoration occurs at the end of the Tribulation period (also known as Jacob's Trouble). Israel will be regathered from the ends of the earth (Isaiah 11:12; 62:10) and be permanently restored to the Land covenanted to them: "I will put My Spirit in you, and you shall live, and I will place you in your own land," (Ezekiel 37:14).

Upon Israel's spiritual restoration, Christ will set up His Kingdom on earth.

> *"Moreover I will make a covenant of peace with them, and it shall be an everlasting covenant with them; I will establish them and multiply them, and I will set My sanctuary in their midst forevermore. My tabernacle also shall be with them; indeed I will be their God, and they shall be My people. The nations also will know that I, the Lord, sanctify Israel, when My sanctuary is in their midst forevermore."*
> Ezekiel 37:26-28

Romans 11:26-27, notably an Old Testament prophecy, is quoted to New Testament believers in Rome:

> *And so all Israel will be saved, as it is written:*
> *"The Deliverer will come out of Zion,*
> *And He will turn away ungodliness from Jacob;*
> *For this is My covenant with them,*
> *When I take away their sins."*

In the Old Testament, the Lord often refers to Israel as a dearly beloved wife, but who was often unfaithful and adulterous. But when Israel returns to the Lord, He will gladly receive her back.

"I will betroth you to Me forever;
Yes, I will betroth you to Me
In righteousness and justice,
In lovingkindness and mercy"
     Hosea 2:19

We also read about this restoration in Jeremiah 31, which we have already considered in light of the New Covenant. But it is helpful to be reminded that this same covenant which the Gentile believer has been grafted into through Christ, mentions the house of Israel and the house of Judah by name, and will be realised when the scales fall and the One who they rejected is embraced as their King of Kings and Lord of Lords.

"Behold, the days are coming, says the Lord, when I will make a new covenant with the house of Israel and with the house of Judah—not according to the covenant that I made with their fathers in the day that I took them by the hand to lead them out of the land of Egypt, My covenant which they broke, though I was a husband to them, says the Lord. But this is the covenant that I will make with the house of Israel after those days, says the Lord: I will put My law in their minds,

and write it on their hearts; and I will be their God, and they shall be My people. No more shall every man teach his neighbour, and every man his brother, saying, 'Know the Lord,' for they all shall know Me, from the least of them to the greatest of them, says the Lord. For I will forgive their iniquity, and their sin I will remember no more."

Heavenly Father, remove any scales from my eyes so that I can see the Truth; remove any veil from my face so that I can see Your Glory; open my heart so that I can sense your Spirit's leading; remove my back's burden so that I can stand in freedom; untangle my feet so that I can run the race with endurance; release my hands so that I can serve and be a blessing; use my tongue so that I can speak with anointing, I surrender my mind so that you can transform my thinking. All that I am, and all that I have, is submitted to Your authority and your power. 'I once was lost, but now I'm free, was blind but now I see'.

Overlooking the Temple Mount,
Jerusalem, Israel

9

As the day approaches

Our understanding of the preparation of the Bride, the Church, is incomplete unless we recognise the function of the Church here on earth until the Bridegroom's return.

The Bible reveals a number of things the Church should be doing specifically 'as the day approaches'. 'The Day' is a Biblical term that encompasses more than one specific day over a period of time. It can refer to the Day when Jesus will rapture His Church from the earth, or the Day of judgement of sinners, or the Day when Jesus will return and set foot on the Mount of Olives, or the Day when Christ will rule from David's throne in Jerusalem. It can also refer to the Day of the Great White Throne Judgement, where the King of kings will separate the sheep and goats, or the Day of the new heaven and new earth, where we will enjoy the presence of the Lord forever. Whilst a comprehensive study of the Last Days informs us of the events connected with Christ's return, it is the commands relating to *preparing* for the Day that I would like to focus on in this chapter.

The following Scriptures mention a specific command associated with the Day approaching. These are not my suggestions. They are what the Bible instructs.

Wake up

Romans 13:11-12 states:

And do this, knowing the time, that now it is high time to **awake out of sleep;** *for now our salvation is nearer than when we first believed. The night is far spent,* **the day is at hand.** *Therefore let us cast off the works of darkness, and let us put on the armour of light.*

Now is not the time for complacency. Now is not the time for compromise. Now is the time to wake up out of sleep. The Church is susceptible to spiritual slumber and is often the reason why she drifts from her first love. The Church cannot be effective if she has closed her eyes forgetting it is day. Spiritual slumber breeds a laziness towards the Truth and an ignorance of darkness. No individual Christian is immune to being overcome by spiritual doziness, but must resist sleeping by putting on the "armour of light".

We read of similar examples. In Matthew 25, five of the ten virgins waiting for the bridegroom were wise and five were foolish. Verse 5 says, "But while the bridegroom was delayed, they all slumbered and slept."

When the cry at midnight announced that the bridegroom was coming, the foolish virgins asked the wise virgins, "Give us some of your oil, for our lamps are going out."

The Holy Spirit has often been depicted as oil in the Bible. We need the Holy Spirit's help to "cast off the works of darkness and put on the armour of light." Denying the Holy Spirit's power expecting to stay spiritually awake is foolishness. On the contrary, spiritual alertness with the Holy Spirit's empowering is wisdom indeed.

Watch

The parable of the foolish and wise virgins ends with the following in verse 11:

"Watch therefore, for you know neither the day nor the hour in which the Son of Man is coming."

Watching is similar to the previous command to stay awake, except watching carries a notion of calling. Like the watchman on the walls of Jerusalem

(Isaiah 62:6), we do not hold our peace "day or night"; we do not keep silent. We remain vigilant to the condition of the world that we live in and to the needs of the generation in which God has ordained us to be placed in. We watch mindful that we have been called out of this world, and we exercise caution that we do not slip into a false sense of comfort.

The Bible warns us of many things that will increase in the Last Days. Although the Church will be preserved from the Great Tribulation, when the Antichrist will temporarily rule before Christ's return, the birth pangs will nonetheless worsen and escalate before the Rapture of the Church.

For example, the Bible tells us to expect the following: there will be false christs, wars and rumours of wars, and nation rising against nation. There will be famines, diseases, false prophets and false teachers; lawlessness, earthquakes, signs in the heavenlies, persecution against Christians across the world, plots against Israel, and a rise in antisemitism. Men's hearts will be full of fear for the future. They will be limited freedoms, including restrictions on foods. They will become more selfish, materialistic, abusive, arrogant and proud. There will be an increase in homosexuality, blasphemy, cold-heartedness, hypocrisy, rebelliousness, ungodliness and lack of respect for authority. There will be a widespread denial of the Creator and truth will be substituted for a lie. False religion will display an appearance of godliness but deny the power of God. More people will be engaged in witchcraft and there will be increase in demonic activity. Greed will increase to a level never seen before, and there will be lack of self-control and increase in self-interest, self-obsession and a self-dependency that denies a dependency on God. There will be a hatred of the truth caused by their love for lust. Sexual immorality will be rife. The depravity is likened to the days of Noah and of Lot, in which God brought judgement, but only after He had made a way of deliverance. There will also be a dramatic shift in world order, in preparation for a one world government under the authority of the Antichrist during the Tribulation (For further reading, see 2 Peter 2:1-3 and 3:1-7; Matthew 24; Mark 13; Luke 21; 1 Timothy 4 and 2 Timothy 3).

The Christian is to remain watchful of these conditions, but not for the following reasons: not to become depressed and weary; not to be doomsayers; not to spread false alarm and fear; not to form a doctrine based on sensationalism and unfounded conspiracy, and not to weaken our testimony.

Instead, one key reason for watching is *to warn*. To warn brothers and sisters of the times and encourage spiritual discernment; to warn the Church so that it remains holy, and to alert the world that Jesus Christ is the way, the truth and the life.

And we must allow our watchfulness to lead us to claim Christ's victory over these things. Our belief that God's Kingdom will prevail over evil should stir us to proclaim, "thy kingdom come, thy will be done, on earth as it is in heaven!"

We should take care not to view these things from an earthly perspective, but with spiritual eyes. As Colossians 3:2 sates, "Set your mind on things above, not on things on the earth."

Furthermore, the signs of the times should provoke us to build anticipation for His return. The Apostle Paul urged Titus, "Looking for the blessed hope and glorious appearing of our great God and Saviour Jesus Christ," (Titus 2:13).

Not all signs are negative. Another sign that we are in the Last Days is the rebirth of the nation of Israel and the repossession of Jerusalem by the Jewish people. The Fig Tree, which is a metaphor for Israel in the Bible (i.e. Hosea 9:10), was the subject of one of Jesus's parables after describing the signs of the times in Matthew 24. The parable tells us that this symbolic tree, cursed for its unfruitfulness, will begin to bud again before Christ's return. The fig tree is one of the last trees to bud in Israel and is a sign that summer is near. Jesus taught that when this tree begins to flourish, it is one of the sure signs that the earth is in the 'Last Days'. In 1948, after 2,000 years dispersed, Israel was reborn as a nation. In 1967, following the Six Day War, the Jewish people regained control of Jerusalem, when it was victorious after being invaded by surrounding nations.

Meanwhile, Isaiah 66:8 has also been associated with the rebirth of the nation of Israel: "Or shall a nation be born at once? For as soon as Zion was in labour, she gave birth to her children." Interestingly, in the previous verse it says, "Before she was in labour, she gave birth before her pain came..." Notice carefully how this analogy is opposite to the birth pangs experienced in natural child birth, which occur in the lead time to the birth and then cease. In Israel's case, this Scripture explains that Zion's birth pangs began *after* she gave birth. In fact, the very next day after nationhood was declared on 14th May 1948, surrounding Arab nations attacked the new-born state. The 'cup of drunkenness' demonstrated by 'surrounding peoples' and those who wish Israel to be 'cut in pieces' and be removed (Zechariah 12:2-3) has continued to this day and are part of Israel's 'post-birth' labour pains as described in Isaiah 66. These events also coincide with the intensifying birth pangs of the Last Days that precede the return of Jesus Christ. This is why the creation of the State of Israel in 1948 has been depicted as the starting trigger of the countdown towards the End Times and the return of Jesus. Additionally, the Jewish people's repossession of Jerusalem is central to God's prophetic clock.

The physical return of the Jewish people to their historic homeland and repossession of their capital, Jerusalem, for the first time in two millennia, can also be considered a visible precursor to the eventual spiritual restoration of Israel that will be fulfilled before Christ's return. After all, we can be confident that Christ is returning to a Jerusalem where Israel is present.

...*"I will gather you from the peoples, assemble you from the countries where you have been scattered, and I will give you the land of Israel.'"*
Ezekiel 11:17

Just as the Bible prophesies about the Land of Israel, the barren desert is again blooming and fruitful since the Jewish people's return.

Even though Israel's troubles are a sure sign of the Last Days, the Bible says that God will comfort Israel and Jerusalem (Isaiah 66:13), and furthermore will defend Israel against her enemies and destroy all the nations that come against Jerusalem (Zechariah 12:8-9). Such is the deep love that God has for Zion, the Bible again uses a bridegroom and bride metaphor, but this time to express a different relationship: His love for Jerusalem:

And as the bridegroom rejoices over the bride,
So shall your God rejoice over you.
I have set watchmen on your walls, O Jerusalem;
They shall never hold their peace day or night.
You who make mention of the Lord, do not keep silent,
And give Him no rest till He establishes
And till He makes Jerusalem a praise in the earth.
Isaiah 62:5b-7

And again in Jeremiah, we read of the voice of the bridegroom rejoicing at the return of the Jewish people to the land of Israel.

*The voice of joy and the voice of gladness, the voice
of the bridegroom and the voice of the bride, the
voice of those who will say:*
  "Praise the Lord of hosts,
  For the Lord is good,
  For His mercy endures forever"—
*and of those who will bring the sacrifice of praise
into the house of the Lord. For I will cause the
captives of the land to return as at the first,' says
the Lord.*
  Jeremiah 33:11

Today, we can look at the existence of Israel and
be reminded that God is faithful to keep His
promises. It is one of the most important
demonstrations that God is moving in these times.
God has allowed the Fig Tree to bear fruit in the Last
Days and we are witnessing it with our eyes.

Psalm 121 tells us that He who watches over
Israel also watches over you. It says that He who
watches over Israel is not sleeping. Let us therefore
watch, confident that God's promises to us
personally, to the Church, and to Israel are firmly
established in His Word.

Witness

Another significant sign of the Last Days is the
preaching of the gospel to the whole earth. How are
we being faithful watchmen if we do not share the
Good News of Jesus to our needy world?

Matthew 28:19 says,

> *"Go therefore and make disciples of all the nations, baptizing them in the name of the Father and of the Son and of the Holy Spirit, teaching them to observe all things that I have commanded you; and lo, I am with you always, **even to the end of the age."** Amen.*

Jesus's instruction to go and make disciples is accompanied by two related promises. Firstly, Christ is with us in this special commission, and secondly He is with us "even to the end of the age." We should interpret this with the understanding that Jesus expected this mission to continue relentlessly for the whole length of time that God has determined.

Prepare

> *For it is impossible for those who were once enlightened, and have tasted the heavenly gift, and have become partakers of the Holy Spirit, and have tasted the good word of God and the powers **of the age to come***
> Hebrews 6:4-5

Notice the phrase "the heavenly gift", and "the powers of the age to come." Both of these are "tasted" or 'sampled' by the regenerated believer, according to this Scripture. We can deduct that believers have been given a foretaste of what will be experienced in "the age to come" through the power of the Holy

Spirit today.

If we think that the gift of the Holy Spirit is for this age alone, we are mistaken. In fact, it is in preparation for eternity. This reminds us of the earlier example of the Helper being sent to prepare the Bride. Every Christian should purpose in their hearts to be transformed by the power of the Holy Spirit. We should want to "taste the heavenly gift" today and ready ourselves for the age to come.

Another way to prepare for eternity is to sow into the things of the Spirit. If we sow to our flesh, we will cultivate things according to our sinful nature. This is unproductive eternally and will actually hinder our spiritual walk today. In contrast, sowing in the Spirit will bear spiritual fruit that will have eternal consequences.

For he who sows to his flesh will of the flesh reap corruption, but he who sows to the Spirit will of the Spirit reap everlasting life.
Galatians 6:8

Thirdly, we prepare for eternity by storing up treasures in Heaven. Jesus said in Matthew 6, "Do not lay up for yourselves treasures on earth, where moth and rust destroy and where thieves break in and steal; but lay up for yourselves treasures in heaven." Jesus explained, "For where your treasure is, there your heart will be also."

As the Bride, we should check what we are setting our affection on. Is our love for the things of the earth, or is our love for the things above? Once we have decided that our love is for the things that are eternal, we should give attention to the "laying up" command of this Scripture. We do this by giving up the cares of this world and the accumulation of worthless investments, and pursue the things that glorify Christ.

Gather

> *"Let us hold fast the confession of our hope without wavering, for He who promised is faithful. And let us consider one another in order to stir up love and good works, not forsaking the assembling of ourselves together, as is the manner of some, but exhorting one another, **and so much the more as you see the Day approaching**."*
> Hebrews 10:24-25

This passage in Hebrews provides us with a very direct instruction to believers not to forsake assembling together. Notice that some had indeed forsaken meeting together, however "exhorting" one another, meaning 'encouraging' one another, is essential not to neglect.

The word "forsaking" is the Greek word *egkataleipo*, which is a compound of the words *ek*, *kata*, and *leipo*. The word *ek* means 'out'; the word *kata* means 'down'; and the word *leipo* means 'to leave or to forsake'. When all three of these words are joined to form a triple-compound word, it carries the meaning of 'abandoning or walking away from something with no intent of returning.'

This is such a strong phrase that stretches beyond simply not attending church regularly, even though attending church is an important routine to practice. Rather, it carries a meaning of permanent abandonment. When we apply it to our verse it reads, 'not completely abandoning and walking away from the assembling of ourselves with no intent of returning.'

But notice the phrase that follows: "and so much more as you see the Day approaching." Here the author of Hebrews makes a direct link to the importance of gathering together that is elevated even further as the Day of the Lord approaches.

Why is this? It suggests that there is an even greater need for members of the Church to gather together in the Last Days, more than at any other time in history. This could be because of an increase in persecution and the necessity of edifying, or 'building up', one another in the faith. The courage of persecuted brothers and sisters worldwide is a humble testimony of living out this verse in a real way. If those living in presently comfortable and free locations are faced with similar circumstances in the future, some may not withstand. But we should pray that God will help us be courageous in following this Scripture if persecution hinders our ability to gather.

The instruction to gather together, especially as the Day approaches, could also be because it is the Lord's will for the Church to multiply in the Last

Days. This is how the early church at the time of Acts grew rapidly and was impactful in the spreading of the Gospel. It was because of the hunger among the Church to gather together in homes and multiply.

But another clue is provided in the same passage: "Let us hold fast the confession of our hope without wavering." It is the Lord's will for you personally, and the Body of Christ collectively, to not waver in our confession of hope. The word for "manner" in the phrase, "as is the manner of some," is the Greek word *ethos*. This word also means 'custom'. God wants His Church to gather together because He wants to prepare the Bride not to waver, but instead to adopt the right 'ethos'. This is the ethos of the Father.

The word for "assembling" is the Greek word *episunagoge*. If you look carefully you will recognise the word 'synagogue' within it. It simply means 'assembly'. And this is the nuanced point in the ethos of gathering together as a Church body. It doesn't say do not forsake 'attendance' as if the Church is something that is simply attended. As Christians, *we* are the Church, the body of believers, the Bride of Christ, and we are to adopt an 'ethos' of 'assembling' together in whatever form or format that might be, or no matter what the location is, or how many people are gathering.

The Bible doesn't say, 'where two or three *attend*'. It says in Matthew 18:20, "For where two or three are gathered together in My name, I am there in the midst of them." And this is the pinnacle of why 'gathering' or 'assembly' is so important. Because

Christ is there in the midst of our gathering together. It is worth not forsaking.

And one day, as if in fulfilment of what is taking place among the Church today, when the Bride of Christ is 'gathered together' in the heavenlies, Christ the Bridegroom shall likewise be in the midst.

Remember

> *...The Lord Jesus on the same night in which He was betrayed took bread; and when He had given thanks, He broke it and said, "Take, eat; this is My body which is broken for you; do this in remembrance of Me." In the same manner He also took the cup after supper, saying, "This cup is the new covenant in My blood. This do, as often as you drink it, in remembrance of Me." For as often as you eat this bread and drink this cup, you proclaim the Lord's death **till He comes**.*
>
> 1 Corinthians 11:23-26

Remembering Jesus's death and resurrection in the Lord's Supper (communion) is a central part of the 'assembling' of ourselves. We've covered this earlier in the book, but notice that we are commanded to do this "till He comes". Every time we take the bread, we remember the body of the Lord Jesus, broken for us. Every time we take the cup, we remember the New Covenant of His blood, shed for the forgiveness of sins. We are reminded of the Covenant that the Bridegroom made with His Bride, the Church. We recognise the price that was paid for our betrothal. And we participate with appreciation that He promised to one day return.

We do this as the Bride for the duration of our separation until the day in which we are in the presence of the Bridegroom. Even then, the Bible doesn't say we will stop partaking – the difference is that when the Bride and the Bridegroom are united, He will be drinking it with us. Hallelujah!

> *"But I say to you, I will not drink of this fruit of the vine from now on until that day when I drink it new with you in My Father's kingdom." And when they had sung a hymn, they went out to the Mount of Olives.*
> Matthew 26:29-30

I am a watchman on the walls. But I am not just an observer. I am a worker for the Kingdom. I am on a mission with a passion for the lost and a burden for my generation and the next. My hope is in the things above, not on the earth. 'The world is passing away, and the lust of it' but I will do the 'will of God which abides forever'. All that I do, I want it to be worthwhile in light of eternity. I want to see Your power manifested in my life and in the Church in these Last Days. Lord, help me stand firm in my faith; to speak the Truth boldly and to be a faithful servant with what You entrust me with. And as I do, may I be an example to those around me, drawing people to Christ and sharing His love.

10

At the feet
of Jesus

The time had almost come. Preparation for the Passover had commenced, but this would be a Passover like no other before. In just a few days, the most defining moment in the history of mankind would take place in Jerusalem.

In a house in Bethany, just outside Jerusalem, a woman named Mary listened intently as Jesus spoke to those who had gathered in Simon the Leper's house.

Jesus had already told his disciples that the time of His death was at hand, but somehow this fact had escaped them, despite Jesus's clear declaration of this truth. But Mary was different. It seems she understood what Jesus had said, either previously, or now as she sat at Jesus's feet. And being 'at His feet' is perhaps the reason why she had this revelation. Because there is nowhere better than at the feet of Jesus.

Spending time at His feet

It wasn't the first time that Mary had been at the feet of Jesus. As her busy sister Martha was distracted serving, it was Mary who "sat at Jesus's feet and heard His word," (Luke 10:39). Jesus responded, "But one thing is needed, and Mary has chosen that good part, which will not be taken away from her," (Luke 10:42).

In John 11, Mary is introduced as "'*that* Mary who anointed Jesus with fragrant oil and wiped His feet with her hair."

When her brother Lazarus had died, it was Mary who rushed to find Jesus, and when she saw Him, "she fell down at His feet" and pleaded with Him (John 11:32). Jesus saw her weeping and "groaned in the spirit and was troubled," before miraculously raising Lazarus from the dead. Despite her perceived quiet disposition, it was through Mary that "many of the Jews that had come" to her "and had seen the things Jesus did, believed in Him," (John 11:45). But others among them went to the Pharisees and complained about Jesus, leading to the plot against Him, such is the splintering impact of the Truth.

Now, for maybe the last time before His imminent

death, Mary was at the feet of Yeshua, hanging onto every word that Her Lord uttered. Fulfilling what Jesus had told her before, she again chose "that good part, which will not be taken away from her."

What Mary did next was not an ordinary traditional greeting or hospitality welcome. In the presence of Jesus, Mary did something astonishing that Jesus prophesied will be told as a memorial to her, wherever the Gospel is preached in the whole world (Mark 14:9).

Mary possessed an alabaster jar containing very expensive oil. The inside the alabaster jar contained spikenard, a very costly ointment that was popular in the Middle East. It was derived from a plant and imported from areas of present-day India, China and Nepal. It was used for medical purposes, as perfume and...for burial.

In Bible times, spikenard was one of the primary ingredients used to prepare bodies for burial. The other ingredient was myrrh. Jesus had already been presented with myrrh. As an infant, of course, it was the Magi that brought myrrh from the east as a gift for the new-born King. Now, three decades later, the final presentation to Jesus was spikenard in preparation for His burial.

In the Song of Solomon, spikenard is mentioned in reference to the love between a bride and groom: "While the king is at his table, my spikenard sends forth its fragrance," (Song of Solomon 1:12). There was a tradition in ancient Israel of Jewish girls being given an alabaster jar containing expensive oil and sealing it in preparation for her future bridegroom. The girl would keep the jar sealed in preparation for her future bridegroom. Then, and only then, would she break open the seal and pour the oil from the alabaster jar at the feet of her beloved.

Bearing this is mind, two pictures now suddenly collide: a bridegroom and a burial.

A bridegroom and a burial

Certainly, Mary, who had been one of the most faithful at being at Jesus's feet during His ministry, remembers hearing about John the Baptist's description of Jesus as Bridegroom. Undoubtedly, Jesus's words about departing to His Father's house, and then returning, resonated with her spirit. Surely, Jesus calling His disciples 'friends of the bridegroom' and Himself as the 'bridegroom' who 'will be taken away from them' (Mark 2:19-22), resonated strongly with the spiritually discerning Mary.

Abraham, Isaac, Lamb, Rebekah, Covenant, Sacrifice, Bridegroom, Betrothal, Cup, Cana, Wedding, Death, Return – suddenly the blueprint unravelled. The time was now. The bridegroom was present. Mary broke the seal.

She didn't just break the seal. The Greek word used for 'break' tells us that she shattered the alabaster jar. It is impossible to place oil back into a smashed jar. The alabaster container could never be used again. It was only for Jesus. It guaranteed every single drop would be poured out for Him. On His head and His feet, Mary poured this precious oil onto her Yeshua.

The fragrance filled the entire house. It was a powerfully symbolic moment.

With the presence of the Bridegroom at the centre of this beautiful act of worship, voices of opposition cut through the atmosphere like a knife. Matthew and Mark say it was some of those present. John names Judas.

"Why was this fragrant oil wasted?" they asked.

Indeed, the fragrance was expensive. It was equivalent to a year's wages. They contended that it would be better spent on the poor.

But when you hear their complaint said aloud, you realise what they really meant, even though they didn't explicitly say it. Reading between the lines, what they *really* meant was, "why waste this fragrance *on Jesus!*"

Jesus rebuked them saying, "Leave her alone...she has kept it for the day of my burial," (John 12:7). Notice the phrase "kept it", mirroring the tradition of keeping the jar for the bridegroom. No wonder Jesus commanded that her faith and her sacrifice would become a testimony throughout the world whenever the gospel is preached.

He is worthy

"Why waste this on Jesus?" – what an insult! Isn't Jesus worthy of our praise? There is nowhere better than at the feet of Jesus. There is no place more wonderful than in His presence. Yet, today there are many who sadly regard such conviction as a waste. It was so during His ministry on earth, and it is so during these days until His reappearing. But I want to encourage you today, that the life dedicated to Jesus is not a waste. The Cross was the defining moment in our struggle with sin. Our old life is passed; we receive the new life given to us by Jesus through faith in Him.

"But what things were gain to me, these I have counted loss for Christ," (Philippians 3:7). This is the heart of the person who believes that Jesus is worthy of our worship – we offer up our lives to His will. He is worthy of it all, so we allow the Holy Spirit to change us and mould us into the person that God has designed us to be for His glory: "I have been crucified with Christ; it is no longer I who live, but Christ lives in me; and the life which I now live in the flesh I live by faith in the Son of God, who loved me and gave Himself for me," (Galatians 2:23).

He gave all for you

If only those who criticised Mary knew the cost of what Jesus was about to do for the broken sinner, then surely they would have accepted that only the best would do.

Just days later, Jesus would die for the sins of the world. The Lord became our Passover Lamb. "This is my body, broken for *you*," He said in the upper room on the night before His crucifixion. Then Jesus takes the cup and gives it to his disciples, but He also sips from the same cup. His sacrifice would become my redemption and His resurrection would become my new life.

Then He became the scapegoat for all humanity. The priests, representing Israel, said 'He must die', deeming the Lamb perfect for sacrifice. But Jesus would not be slain for the house of Israel alone. Representing the Gentile nations, Rome's Pilate declared, "I find no fault in this Man." Even Jesus's betrayer Judas lamented, "I have sinned by betraying innocent blood." The perfect Lamb was certified, and He was delivered to the people who shouted "crucify Him" in exchange for a sinner's release.

"Eli, Eli, lama sabachthani?", "My God, My God, why have You forsaken Me?" our Lord cried as He bore the weight of our transgressions on the Cross. Although He was without any sin, He was fully obedient to the Father, willingly humbled Himself, and became sin for us on the Cross.

It is finished

Once a year the High Priest entered the Holy of Holies, taking the blood of the lamb for the day of atonement. The people waited outside in silence to find out whether the sacrifice was acceptable to God. At that very hour, Jesus cried on Calvary, "It is finished!" At that moment, the earth shook and daytime turned to darkness; the veil (curtain) in the Temple separating the Holy of Holies from the Holy

Place split in two from top to bottom. 'It is finished'. The last sacrifice of the old covenant was made, the New Covenant burst forth. Previously, fear of death would overwhelm any person who had sight of the Holy of Holies and Ark of the Covenant, but not on this memorable day. The people lived. The sacrifice was perfect. The separation between them and God was removed by the blood of the Lamb of God, 'who takes away the sins of the world'.

Death and darkness shrouded the earth, but on the third day, Jesus rose again. His heel was bruised, but Satan's head was crushed as He defeated sin and death by being victorious over the grave. Just days after Mary's outpouring of oil on Jesus's feet in preparation for His burial, her Lord was now risen from the dead. The debt of her sin and our sin was paid. Just as He had said, "I am the resurrection and the life. He who believes in Me, though he may die, he shall live," (John 11:25).

No wonder He is worthy of our worship. No wonder He deserves the outpouring of ourselves before Him.

New life in Jesus

We serve a living Saviour, who loves us and gave Himself for us. The life that we now have, we live through Christ Jesus. But it is a life that has been changed. The Bible says that if anyone is in Christ "he is a new creation; old things have passed away; behold, all things have become new," (2 Cor 5:17).

The Bible says in Ephesians 3:17,

> *"That Christ may dwell in your hearts through faith; that you, being rooted and grounded in love, may be able to comprehend with all the saints what is the width and length and depth and height— to know the love of Christ which passes knowledge; that you may be filled with all the fullness of God."*

Jesus Christ loves you, and He is calling *you* into relationship with Him today. My prayer is that you will be confident in the certainty that God keeps all His promises. His Word *will* come to pass.

> *"Eye has not seen, nor ear heard,*
> *Nor have entered into the heart of man*
> *The things which God has prepared for those who love Him."*
> 1 Corinthians 2:9

God has a special plan for you, in the present and into eternity with Jesus. This is our blessed hope.

Until the Lord calls us home or returns for His Bride, may we do what God has called us to do today: be ready for His return and faithfully listen to the voice of the Bridegroom.

Thank you, Lord, for Your great love for me. Thank you for what You did on the Cross, by dying for me. I repent of my sins and ask You to forgive me. I am saved by the blood of Jesus. I am forgiven. I have been purchased back. I have been reconciled back to God. I believe in the resurrection of Jesus Christ and receive with gladness the new life You have given me. I will not be defined by my old sinful nature. I leave that at the Cross. I am a new creation and will claim the promises of this new life. The life I now live I live for Jesus. May it be poured out before you as an offering of worship. You are worthy of all my praise. I know that your Spirit is with me and that you will return. I pray that I will listen to the voice of the Bridegroom all the days of my life.

Printed in Great Britain
by Amazon

39015622R00089